A MUSICIAN'S GUIDE TO THE ROAD

A MUSICIAN'S GUIDE TO THE ROAD

by Gary Burton

A BILLBOARD BOOK
AN IMPRINT OF WATSON-GUPTILL PUBLICATIONS/NEW YORK

Copyright © 1981 by Gary Burton

First published 1981 in New York by Billboard Books,
an imprint of Watson-Guptill Publications,
a division of Billboard Publications, Inc.,
1515 Broadway, New York, N.Y. 10036

Library of Congress Cataloging in Publication Data

Burton, Gary.
  A musician's guide to the road.

  (A Billboard book)
  Includes index.
  1. Music—Economic aspects. 2. Business travel.
I. Title.
ML3795.B93   910'.2478   80-27182
ISBN 0-8230-7583-4

All rights reserved. No part of this publication may be
reproduced or used in any form or by any means—graphic,
electronic, or mechanical, including photocopying, recording,
taping, or information storage and retrieval systems—without
written permission of the publisher.

Manufactured in U.S.A.

First Printing, 1981

Were I to pick a subject on which to write, travel life would not have been my first thought. However, over the years, I have been contacted so often by fellow musicians and people in the music business to find out about the endless details involved in getting a band from one place to another that I have come to feel I might be offering a valuable contribution with this book.

I would like to respectfully dedicate this to the two friends who taught me the most about the subject: Ed Fuerst, whom I first met in 1963 with George Shearing's group, and Charles Bourgois, with George Wein's production company in New York.

I must extend thanks to Peggy Dunn, who provided tremendous assistance in the preparation of the original manuscript. My thanks also to my wife, Cricket, and my friend Ted Kurland, who pushed me to finally finish the project.

I also wish to thank Greta Moses, my travel agent for many years, a wonderful friend and a constant source of information and positive spirit.

Gary Burton

CONTENTS

FOREWORD   9

1. HOW TO GET THERE   13
From finding a good travel agent to arriving at your destination—whether it be via plane, train, bus, or rental car, truck, or trailer—every detail about reservations, tickets, and rates is covered.

2. GETTING THE EQUIPMENT THERE   53
Choosing cases, taking them with you, and getting through customs—all the possible tangles—what to do to make sure your equipment gets there the same (or nearly the same) time you do.

3. WHERE TO STAY   61
Deciding where to stay, along with what to expect from reservations and rates, and how to smoothly check in and out—all the special factors musicians, with their erratic schedules, should consider.

4. HOW TO COPE WITH THE GIG   77
Knowing what to expect from agents, managers, and promoters, getting paid for the gig, the invaluable checklist system, and renting and repairing equipment on tour.

5. THINGS TO SIMPLIFY YOUR LIFE ON TOUR   93
Making sure your monetary and communications needs are taken care of on tour (especially foreign), keeping road expense reports, the all-important carnet, and dealing with the local musician's union.

6. CREDIT, LOANS, AND INSURANCE FOR MUSICIANS AND OTHER UNSAVORY CHARACTERS   113
Working with and around the worlds of credit and insurance—where musicians are often unwelcome—to get full convenience and benefits for yourself and your tour.

APPENDIXES   123
A. Checklists
B. Samples of Touring Forms
C. Useful Books and Addresses
D. Sample Contracts
E. Carnet Information

INDEX   155

FOREWORD

It is one of the unavoidable facts about a musical career that a certain amount of travel is likely to be necessary. This should never be confused with vacation travel or even regular business travel. For the musician, traveling early in the day means not getting enough sleep after last night's gig, and traveling late in the day means not having time to eat dinner before tonight's gig. Plus traveling with a group of musicans—people we might charitably describe as extremely eccentric—day after day, in close quarters, and with a ton of equipment and luggage is not conducive to a fun trip, nor is it anything resembling a vacation.

I've been touring regularly for about twenty years since 1960, and though I don't presume to be an expert on everything concerning travel, I do offer what knowledge I have to those facing the same fate.

To be sure, conditions have improved markedly since the arrival of the jet age and the advent of interstate highways, but I'll never forget the seedy hotels, prop planes, and incredibly slow trips of earlier times. Possibly one of the best improvements since the sixties is in race relations. On the first tours I made in racially mixed groups it was difficult in the South to put all the musicians in the same hotel, and in some towns it was necessary for black musicians to stay in local homes because hotels weren't even available to them. In 1963, a roadside restaurant became infamous in my mind for serving coffee to the white band members in china cups and to the blacks in paper ones. Holiday Inns broke the dam on this problem when they appeared in the mid-sixties with a strict, nondiscrimination policy. They made travel in the South a dignified possibility at last. I've remained somewhat partial to Holiday Inns ever since for this reason.

Foreign travel adds several new dimensions, of course. My first foreign tour in 1960 prepared me for just about anything. It was a month's tour of South America on a tight budget. We flew on Ini (pronounced Ee-nee) Airlines, which should have been called "Teeny Airlines" (or something worse). The airline had only two prop planes: a DC-6 and a DC-4. On the 30-hour trip to Argentina, I encountered my first language barrier. An elderly gentleman tripped over my foot as he shuffled down the aisle and fell flat on his face—and was out cold on the floor. I started to tell someone, but was struck by the fact that not a single person, including the stewardesses, spoke English and I spoke no Spanish. I had visions of being held for protracted investigations into the death of this poor man, so in a burst of monumental confusion I sat down and pretended I didn't know anything about it. Every few minutes I would glance around to see if he was still there—he was, and not moving a muscle. I just knew he had died. What now, I thought. Finally someone noticed him and the stewardess slowly revived him with oxygen. I was practically ready for the oxygen myself by that time—and feeling pretty guilty.

The tour itself was full of surprises (not the least of which was the disappearance of our promoters), but none so memorable as the return trip. We were informed that our departure would be delayed because of repairs to the plane. I asked how long. They said they would call our hotel in a few days to let us know! So we waited—checking into a hotel in Buenos Aires and watching our money trickle away. Our hotel cost $1.50 a day for a double (we got a discount from the $2 rate because we were the only guests who stayed all night and brought luggage). We spent five days there. Entertainment was limited to walking around the streets, sitting at local clubs, and finally each night running the gauntlet of hotel ladies when we went back to our rooms.

The trip back on Ini's smaller plane took 36 hours. We had to use oxygen masks when we flew over the Andes. The plane stopped every four or five hours to refuel and pick up another load of cold chicken dinners. After four consecutive cold chicken dinners it was a long time before I could face a chicken again.

I arrived back home to Newbury Street in Boston with 25 cents left, and I would like to say a *lot* wiser, but probably only a little more so. I did have the time of my life, however. Thank god I was only eighteen!

I also discovered how foreign customs work and how wonderful some people can be too. Our instruments never caught up with us on our tour, but instead collected dust in Argentine customs houses for a couple months. I finally located my vibraphone once I returned home and did something I wouldn't dream of doing now. I sent several hundred dollars to a nearly total stranger to arrange to ship my instrument home. And he, being a true prince, took care of it all and sent me the $10 change that was left over.

Foreign languages and local customs are always a curious treat too. On one occasion in 1968, bassist Steve Swallow and I accompanied Barney Kessel, the guitarist, to a local restaurant in Dusseldorf, Germany. Barney was proud of having learned some German and insisted on ordering for us all. The waiter looked a little perplexed and protested slightly, but Barney persisted. As the waiter left, Barney suddenly remembered he had placed a phone call to California and rushed back to the hotel, leaving Steve and me to our dinner. Shortly, the waiter brought seven huge steins of beer and set them on the table before us. We laughed for days and never did tell Barney about it. Once, on a tour to Japan, one of the equipment handlers was an hour late for a departure because he overslept. The next day we noticed the same fellow at the hotel several hours early. We asked the promoter why he was so early and he very matter-of-factly answered that he was making up for being late the day before. Something different, huh?

Another foreign adventure I wouldn't care to repeat took place in Bangkok, Thailand, a normally enchanting locale, I'm sure. I was there in 1966 with Stan Getz for a function honoring then-President Lyndon Johnson and the King of Thailand, a saxophonist himself and jazz fan.

My hotel room was unusual in the extreme. Instead of having no hot water, I had no cold water! Both faucets put out scalding hot water at all times of the day. To take a bath, I had to fill the tub and then wait at least half an hour for it to cool down. Brushing my teeth was an even greater problem. And then, there were my roommates. About half a dozen lizards were attached to the walls and ceiling. On the first day, I painstakingly captured each one and took them outside; but that night I returned to find even more of them all over the room. I stopped resisting them at that point. It sure was eerie, though. Later, I learned that they were supposed to bring good luck.

The night of the performance for the dignitaries started with a banquet in the tropical heat of the palace function hall. At first, it went well enough, but as dessert was served disaster struck. The waiter was dishing out strawberry ice cream from a huge tureen. Unfortunately it had become strawberry soup because of the heat, and as he leaned over to serve the lady to my right, he leaned too far and about two gallons of molten ice cream glopped into my lap, turning my white tuxedo jacket into an interesting experiment in pink. Then, I stood up with such a start that I ripped the seat out of my too-tight tuxedo pants. Before anything else could happen, word arrived that we were due on stage immediately. Just what I needed! But I did make it through without turning around or getting permanently stuck to anything that wasn't my own.

When I finally got back to my room, I sat for an hour with the "lucky" lizards waiting for the bath water to cool so I could at last say good-bye to the strawberry ice cream. What a way to earn a living!

It seems to me that the trick to surviving road life is to be able to enjoy the bizarre and the unusual and to turn the disasters into adventures. I'm not always so good at this myself, as numerous fellow travelers through the years could testify, but I offer it as a prescription for a happy life on the road. In addition, be as prepared as possible and the last-minute problems will be smaller and more manageable. That's what this book is supposed to help accomplish.

In order to protect myself against the material in this book becoming obsolete before it even comes off the presses, I would like to point out that the ravages of inflation and high energy costs have made constant changes in the price of travel. In addition, types of fare structuring, particularly with plane travel, seem to be changing rapidly in an effort to keep up with the monetary changes.

So please take into account that examples of dollar figures for fares, rates, etc., may not be accurate in the near future. I have intentionally tried to state such information in a generalized way with this in mind. Given the speed of changes in prices lately, the figures I am using may soon be grossly underestimated.

Gary Burton
Chestnut Hill, Massachusetts
1980

CHAPTER 1

HOW TO GET THERE

TRAVEL AGENTS

Travel agents serve an invaluable purpose for the traveler, with few limitations. And the service they provide is the rarest of all things—something that is free. The travel agent has the latest airline guide books giving all scheduled flights and can make reservations and issue tickets just as if you were at a ticket counter at the airport. In addition, the experienced travel agent knows a lot of miscellaneous information about many cities, hotels, and travel alternatives so he or she can offer assistance far beyond the efforts of the usual airline office.

For booking foreign tours with several stops, a travel agent is really essential. There are a maze of alternate schedules and ways of computing international fares that take the expertise and perseverance of a travel agent to sort out. Certainly relying on an airline would not be likely to turn up the best deals, and the difference saved could be in the hundreds of dollars. For this reason alone everyone should understand that the travel agent deserves a sympathetic attitude from the customer. Plus, most function as a sort of independent operator, working on a commission basis shared with their office. The commissions from airlines, hotels, or rental car companies are not substantial, so that sales of individual tickets are not a major profit item for them. Most agents concentrate on group vacation tours for their major business. The current travel agent commission is 7 percent of the ticket price on airline tickets, although now some airlines have switched to paying a flat rate of $8 per ticket, which may become the standard in the future. Hotels and other businesses such as auto rentals usually pay 10 percent commissions to the agents. You can easily compute that this does not amount to a large sum on a short trip for one individual.

FINDING A GOOD AGENT

Many agents I have encountered have found a musician's special requirements annoying. Foremost among the problems of a traveling group of musicians are the occasional last-minute changes in itinerary, causing frantic rebooking of reservations and tickets. Also music groups often have unbelievable baggage requirements (large instruments or an unwillingness to be parted from them, etc.) which make for complications in advance arrangements with the airlines. In picking an agent, try to find one that shows an interest in giving personal attention and service, as well as a readiness to work with these special requirements. Obviously, an agent who is a music fan is a big plus.

If you know any musicians who already use a travel agent, try their agent first since they will already be broken in and acquainted with a musician's way of operating. A good opening with a new agent is to offer to pay cash on the spot the first time or two when purchasing tickets. With an obvious cash sale, you'll be readily received. A few dealings of this sort should establish you sufficiently as a customer and entitle you thereafter to pay by check and be billed for the tickets.

The main thing to remember is to pay your travel agent *before* you travel and not use their services as a form of credit or delayed purchase. Many agents are cautious about having musicians as clients: tours *can* go broke and they have heard "Your check is in the mail" numerable times without anything materializing. You'll soon lose their cooperation if you take advantage of them. Unfortunately, the system itself encourages abuse of travel agents because they must pay the charges to the airline in full a short time after the ticket is issued: if they have trouble collecting from a client, their own money gets tied up. For a first-time customer the agency might well insist on a check clearing before the tickets are turned over. If you need 30 days to pay for your travel, you'll have to have credit cards. (See Paperwork in Chapter 5.)

AIRLINES

Even if you use a travel agent, there will be times when you'll need to deal directly with airline personnel, such as when making last-minute changes during a trip. So it's a good idea to know the airlines' reservations procedures, special circumstances, and last-minute surprises. Many times I've observed airline personnel misleading customers or failing to point out important information. Knowing the airline methods is to be forewarned.

RESERVATION PROCEDURES
One of the most successful uses of computer technology is the airline reservation and ticketing system. The airline operator projects the necessary flight information onto a screen and makes bookings directly through the computer, which keeps an up-to-date list

of the expected passengers. Reservations can be changed to alternative flights with the ease of typing the information into the computer. So it is usually a quick and easy process.

In most cities reservation phone lines are staffed 24 hours a day, and some airlines have a central toll-free number covering several states which offers 24-hour service as well.

When you call an airline to inquire about the availability of service from one city to another, the reservationist will tell you immediately if they don't serve that city and will suggest the other airlines that do. However, if they do serve the route you want, their policy is to first tell you only about their particular flights. They, of course, would rather put you on one of their flights instead of that of another airline, even if their service isn't the most convenient. If you want to know about alternative flights with another line, you'll have to ask about it directly and not expect them to volunteer any information. Just say, "Do any other carriers have service on this route?" Only if a company's flights are sold out will they check alternatives and book you on the other company's plane.

TIP

If there's a crisis in your city and the reservation phone lines of the airline are jammed, try picking another city served by that airline and call that reservation number long distance. All reservation offices can make reservations for any flight in their route system.

CLASS OF SERVICE
Most domestic air travel is done at full fare rates with a choice between tourist (or coach) class and first class. There is also the so-called standard class on short-flight airlines, which is sort of the same as coach nowadays.

First class is about one-third more expensive than tourist (on domestic flights) but offers various extras such as large, comfortable seats, less crowding, better meal service (particularly on longer flights), and generally much more attention from the serving crew.

Most people fly tourist for economic reasons—for the many special discount fares that are available. Not all discount possibilities are practical for the business traveler, but there will be times when money can be saved by meeting the discount fare requirements. More about special fare rates later in this chapter.

Discount fares are especially valuable for European travel and are usually offered as some sort of excursion fare, providing a considerable savings over full fare. First class travel around Europe (approximately double the cost of tourist) is so infrequently used these days that an increasing number of flights within Europe no longer offer that service.

Some international flights are also offering a so-called business class for full-fare coach passengers, or something slightly more expensive than coach. This provides certain amenities—better food, free drinks, free movie, separate seating section from the discount travelers for more privacy and less crowding.

SPECIAL FARE RATES

Occasionally it's possible to realize considerable savings through a special rate. The airlines' latest trend is to offer a great variety of discount flights, with various restrictions in travel times, number of days during the trip, advance reservations, etc. With these restrictions not all discount fares will be practical for the business traveler; however, here are a few of the different types of fares available and their main features. Keep in mind that the rules of the game change constantly, and ask your travel agent or airline representative for the latest requirements.

Super-Saver or Excursion Fares: These fares apply to round trip travel between two cities and represent a considerable savings for the traveler (from 20 percent to 50 percent less than full coach fare). The ticket must be purchased from seven to thirty days in advance (depending on the circumstances) and usually requires one week's stay, sometimes less. In some cases, a Friday night included within the stay is all that is required.

European excursion fares are similar, but don't always mean major savings if you want to add additional stopovers. European full fares are based on the distance to the farthest point. You are allowed as many stopovers in other cities as you want as long as it is within a certain mileage limit. You begin paying extra after your total air mileage allotment is used up.

Air travel within Europe is extremely expensive if the ticket is purchased there. The transatlantic ticket, purchased in the U.S., allows much cheaper travel within Europe.

One important note: advance purchases, super-saver, and excursion fares prohibit you from changing your ticket at the last minute. In such a case, you would have to pay the full-fare rate.

Nightcoach: If you can travel after nine at night and before eight in the morning, you can sometimes save as much as 30 percent of the regular fare. This choice is not offered on all flights between all cities—check to make sure.

Standby: The greatest bargain since World War II is the low-cost international standby fare. With some variations, the airlines offer a number of seats on certain flights at extremely low fares. If you have a flexible schedule and are able to avoid traveling on hectic holiday travel days, then you might be able to take advantage of this good opportunity. The airlines are opening up more cities on a standby basis all the time.

TIP

There are a number of special discount fares with varying restrictions. For instance, Eastern has been offering a flat rate for unlimited travel on their route system during a 7-to-21-day period. For about $650 (the current rate) you can travel anywhere at any time during the specified period as long as you stay on Eastern flights.

Other bargains are often available in the form of one-time special fares. An airline wishing to increase customer awareness of a new route may choose to offer substantial discounts (perhaps 50 percent or more) for a month or two. I have occasionally stumbled onto one of these bargains by calling three or four airlines which serve a particular route to get their prices. The smaller airlines seem most likely to hold these special sales, and it's usually when there are several airlines competing for the business on the same route.

Price wars between airlines also bring about rock-bottom fares on some routes from time to time. Keep reminding your travel agent that you want to take advantage of bargain fares, and the agent will probably turn up a regular choice of possibilities for you.

Waiting-List Standby: When you call for a reservation and find out that a flight is totally booked in the tourist section, you will be offered the option of paying extra to fly first class. You can be wait-listed for tourist, and if seats open up, you will automatically be moved into tourist. If both classes of service are sold out, then you might be asked if you want to join a standby list to get on the flight.

A list is begun in the order of the passengers calling in for seats, and as passengers fail to show for the flight in the last 10 minutes or so before departure, the extra seats are filled with the standby passengers. The airline will tell you if you are near the top of the list, and if so, your chances are pretty good for getting on. The odds decrease considerably if you're farther down the list—too much anxiety for me and very unreliable when traveling with a group. An individual traveling alone can usually get on, but for a group of several people, it's unlikely you'll all make it.

PURCHASING TICKETS

Cash is always welcome, of course, at a ticket counter or in town airline office. And you can usually pay by check and always by credit card. The airlines are not required to accept checks, but fortunately, unlike many other types of businesses, they still honor checks on most occasions. But be prepared to offer solid identification. If you pay by check or credit card also be prepared for the fact that large sums almost always require a call to your bank for verification or the credit card company for approval. A bonus for credit card users: some companies automatically include flight insurance at no additional charge. (See the section on credit cards in Chapter 5.)

PREPAY TICKETS

When the ticket is purchased, the buyer can request that it be a paid-for ticket to be made available at *any* airport. In last-minute situations or when purchasing a ticket for someone in another city, this for you—with an exception: if it is for a departure from the agent's home city, the prepaid ticket can only be issued the day of departure.

It takes a minimum of thirty minutes—sometimes longer—after

the purchase before the ticket is available at the airport for pick up, and if it is a complicated itinerary, the actual writing up could take up to several hours. When picking up *any* unusual ticket, allow at least an hour before flight time and more if you expect the airport to be crowded. I once stood in line in the TWA terminal at New York's Kennedy Airport for over an hour trying to pick up a prepaid ticket on a summer weekend. TWA was vying for some of Freddie Laker's Sky Train customers with a standby offer of their own and there were lots of takers. I only made my plane because it was late.

Remember: Proofread your tickets when you collect them or you might find yourself with an unusable ticket far away from home. On the same trip that began at the TWA terminal, my ticket was prepared hurriedly and incorrectly, so that when I later wanted to have it changed, I couldn't because the original ticket was so full of errors. One portion of the trip was missing from the ticket entirely, forcing me to pay several hundred dollars for a separate ticket to cover the missing portion.

PICKING UP TICKETS

If you call in your reservation to an airline, the final phase of the discussion will be about picking up your ticket. On short notice tickets are usually available at the airport ticket counter at least one hour prior to flight time. (At peak travel times, holiday weekends, etc., you would be well advised to allow an hour and a half—or more—at the larger airports which often get jammed.) If time permits, tickets may be mailed to the customer or claimed at an intown airline office. On some flights the airline may set a date for cancellation if the tickets aren't picked up and paid for by that time.

EXCHANGE OF TICKETS

One big advantage of airline tickets is that they are customarily interchangeable from one airline to another. If you want to switch to a different airline to take a more convenient flight at the last minute, the ticket can usually be rewritten or revalidated quite simply when you check in for the flight.

There are a few notable exceptions, though. If the ticket is booked as part of a charter group or excursion fare, then it is generally required that you at least stay with the airline which issued the ticket originally. Also, on international flights, tickets are not automatically exchangeable between airlines. For example, a ticket purchased from Pan American for a return flight on their airline cannot be readily changed so you can come home on a Swissair flight instead. To do this Pan Am would have to "endorse" the ticket over to the competing airline. Ticket agents don't want to be difficult (although I've sometimes thought it might be a hiring prerequisite), but it is their policy to only change a ticket if the reason is a compelling one. If you're desperate to switch, it wouldn't hurt to have a persuasive story. I've used various ones, such as a medical emergency at home, death of a relative, or concert date that will be missed unless I can make a particular flight. Anything is better than not having a specific reason, which will almost ensure your being refused. An exchange can take from several hours to a day or two for the ticket to be rewritten if you have to reroute or if it must be recalculated in the case there is a fare difference.

TIP

Don't presume a complicated ticket can be instantly changed at the counter. Check on it ahead of time and you won't get hung up.

LOST TICKETS AND REFUNDS

An unused ticket can be refunded quite quickly by an airline although not always in cash. In general practice a check is mailed to your home within a few days after you turn in the ticket, or a check is issued at the ticket counter if you bring it in yourself. A ticket issued by a travel agent or paid for through a credit card account will have the refund sent directly to the agency or credit card company.

Partially used tickets take an extraordinary amount of time for refund. I have noticed, in fact, that the refund time on these tickets seems to get longer and longer. It can take as long as three or four months, particularly if it is an international ticket. It is a nuisance to wait several months for a refund of perhaps several hundred dollars. Hopefully, the regulatory agencies will eventually set some time limit for this which is fairer for the customer.

TIP

If you have an expensive ticket and find you're only going to use one portion of it and have to submit the rest for a refund, you might prefer not to use the ticket at all. Pay for your flight with a check or credit card, and then get a quick refund on the completely unused ticket. It's the partially used tickets that seem to take so long for refunds.

A lost ticket is another matter: since tickets are almost like cash—if you've lost it, it's gone. You can only hope for a refund, and in the meantime pay for a replacement ticket. The claiming procedure involves filling out a lost ticket application, submitting it to the airline, and then suffering through a four-month wait while the airline sees if the original ticket gets used by anyone before coming across with a refund.

TIP

Although it might seem like a nuisance to do it, the smart traveler should make a note of the airline ticket number on his ticket, particularly in the case of an expensive, complicated one, so that in case of loss, you could report the ticket number to the airline for speedier tracing and checking.

CHECKING IN FOR THE FLIGHT
This can take place at the ticket counter or at the gate if your ticket doesn't need to be changed in any way. This is simply a matter of the ticket agent telling the computer that you have arrived for the flight. Next you will be given a boarding pass and sometimes an advance seat selection. I give obtaining a boarding pass priority over doing other things in the terminal even if I have to walk a distance to the gate, for without it there is no guarantee of getting on

the plane. In a case of overbooking, those with the first boarding passes get the seats. For passengers traveling together, it's sometimes possible to reserve groups of seats in advance. Call ahead and inquire.

Many airlines have a policy of canceling your seat 10 to 20 minutes before flight time if you haven't checked in by that time. Incidentally, several times I've encountered airlines changing the flight departure to an *earlier*-than-scheduled time! A couple of years ago I checked in with Swissair in Zurich and found out that my 1:00 o'clock flight had left at 11:00 A.M. because of an air controllers' strike. Another time in Milan, Italy, I missed a flight because they automatically move all departures up 1 hour whenever the airport has fog (to allow time to bus the passengers to another airport away from the fog). On that occasion, three bands missed their flight and their concerts. The airline simply said that everybody knows that when there's fog in Milan, the departure is 1 hour earlier!

This past year I had a flight time moved earlier by fifteen minutes just before takeoff for some unexplained reason. The members of the group who were eating in the coffee shop barely made it because the change happened after we had checked in and gotten our boarding cards and all. Never be too complacent about making a flight or you may miss one and miss a concert as well.

CHECKING IN YOUR BAGGAGE

Officially, on domestic flights a passenger is allowed two pieces of luggage of average size and weight. Oversized pieces or more than two pieces per person usually incur an excess baggage charge of so much per extra piece. Currently it is $7 per extra piece and $14 or more per oversized piece. On international flights to or from a U.S. city, the same two-piece system applies. However, the amount charged for extra pieces is substantial. Each extra piece on a flight between New York and Frankfurt, for instance, is approximately $85!

On international flights that don't involve U.S. cities, such as flights around Europe, the international baggage allowance is 44 pounds per passenger in tourist and 66 pounds for first class, with excess charged at a rate based on 1 percent of the first class fare per kilo of excess weight.

Instruments weighing hundreds of pounds can become almost prohibitively expensive to take as excess baggage, and this is one of the major expenses for musical groups touring in foreign countries.

The excess baggage rules are rather strictly followed in Europe and other foreign countries. Carry-on bags, always limited to one on international flights, are supposed to be included in your baggage allowance, but most airlines won't bother counting them as part of your weight allowance.

In the United States excess baggage procedures are very loose. Ninety percent of the time excess charges can be avoided by using the curbside check-in. Even at the counter inside the terminal excess pieces are often overlooked. It depends little on the individual airline's policy and mostly on the employees. The skycap isn't authorized to charge you excess and would have to take you inside the terminal for this. It's better to try to encourage him not to go through the bother. It's definitely easier for him to simply check your items directly and get on with his other work; so to help him make his decision, it doesn't hurt to be nice to him. Have your ticket ready to show him, have the pieces all properly labeled, and let him know that you understand how much work it will be if he has to take oversized pieces down to the loading area by hand because they won't fit in the conveyor systems.

It's my experience that a ready tip for the skycap will help influence his decision. I usually stand there conspicuously holding the money I intend to give him for a tip. If there are a number of pieces, including some heavy ones, then a $10 or $20 bill is a fair amount (50¢ to $1 for each piece). Better to overtip than to undertip; after all, if the skycap saves you from being charged excess baggage fees, you might save more than the $10 or $20 tip. And you'll need the skycap's services anyway, if you have a lot of things. In some cases this won't work and the skycap will take you inside for a check-in anyway. Even still, the counter agent may not charge you excess either. At least 50 percent of the time, nothing is charged, it seems.

Sometimes the skycaps are under strict orders from the counter supervisor to bring in excess baggage for charging and the skycap will have no choice. Play along, hope for the best, and feel good every time you are able to avoid having to pay the extra cost.

Unfortunately, as airline profits get squeezed by fuel costs and tight competition, the airlines tend to step up collection of excess baggage fees.

Occasionally a skycap or counter agent will want you to take your equipment over to the air freight terminal. This rarely occurs, but the three or four times it has happened to me have been more than enough. Not only will you probably not be able to get the equipment on the same flight as you're flying on, but you also will have to wait for a couple of hours to claim it at the air freight terminal upon arrival.

Another method to possibly avoid air freight for a mass of heavy baggage is to call the airline and let them know in advance to expect it. There is a 70-pound-per-piece maximum weight allowed (62 pounds on TWA) and size limits that vary from one airline to another (usually the length of a set of skis, for instance).

A new regulation I just recently noticed on a United Air Lines ticket envelope was a statement that baggage numbering more than four pieces in excess per person (or a total of six pieces) will be charged four times the excess bag rate! I've never traveled with more than six bags per person, but it could happen and the charges would be exorbitant. And I don't know if it is a policy on other airlines or just on United. Each airline sets its own guidelines regarding baggage.

Carry-on luggage is not usually counted by the skycap although it is supposed to be part of your baggage allowance. Carrying aboard small instruments, such as horns and guitars, which are beyond the carry-on size limits is strictly a matter of choice with the airline employees. More than half the time if you are inconspicuous with your oversized item, nothing will be said. But you never know when you will run into a curmudgeon sticking to the letter of the law who would even insist upon a concert violinist checking his priceless instrument with the baggage or forcing him to take another flight.

I have heard of many approaches to this problem. One for guitars is to put it inside a garment bag and hang it in the plane's coat closet. Not all planes have hanging space for garment bags, but most do. Just don't let a stewardess take it from you to kindly hang it up or she'll know what's up.

Incidently, Canadian airports are extremely conscientious about carry-on size limits—to the point of having a metal frame that your carry-on must pass through in order to be allowed on the plane.

Of course, an extra seat can be purchased for half-fare on domestic flights and full fare on international flights (no excursion fare available either) for large instruments. This is expensive but often necessary with a cello or bass, etc. However, it is still possible on fully booked flights for the instrument to be refused its seat in favor of a human being wanting to travel on that flight. It's the option of the airline crew.

The deciding factor regarding oversized pieces in the flight cabin is actually the captain and the crew, not the airline policy. The rules are there for all, but enforcement varies widely. Some want to help us get where we are going with respect for our beloved instruments, and others are on a personal power trip and delight in enforcing the rules in every case, no matter what.

There is also checking of fragile items at the gate. This way your instrument is spared the conveyor belt system and is loaded directly into the baggage compartment from the gate. You can also claim it at the gate when the plane arrives at your destination. Just ask if this service is offered.

ALTERNATIVES FOR OVERSIZED EQUIPMENT
In an effort to ease problems at check-in counters (and to make additional freight revenue), some airline counter employees will refuse to check anything larger than ordinary suitcases and instead insist upon sending it as air freight. Their idea is that you should check the pieces at the freight terminal *one day in advance* and then upon arrival wait for a couple of hours more to claim them at the air freight terminal. We all hope the obvious unpopularity of this scheme will make it short-lived.

If your baggage is definitely too massive and awkward for ordinary checking, you may have to use air freight unless you can make advance arrangements with the company for your extra baggage requirements. Don't assume anything. (See Air Freight in Chapter 2.)

═══════════════ TIP ═══════════════

Because of bumps and knocks, most travelers are wise to use plastic instead of glass bottles, but for additional protection I put my containers of shampoo and other liquids inside plastic bags. I have become a leading advocate of this approach after I opened my suitcase on an arrival in Europe and found everything covered with green, sticky shampoo. The changes in air pressure in baggage compartments can cause even tightly closed containers to leak.

KINDS OF LUGGAGE
I have a few suggestions regarding the different types of luggage available. Essentially you have a choice between rigid, formed lug-

gage, such as Samsonite, which offers excellent protection for the contents but tends to have limited wearing time before the locks cease to function or the frame gets bent beyond use; or soft-sided, zippered luggage, such as Lark, which offers less protection for the contents but seems to wear for years, absorbing bumps and knocks. My favorite is the Halliburton Company aluminum suitcase, with heavy-duty locks, that is sturdy and reliable—but also more expensive. Their suitcases are available in major luggage stores throughout the United States. It seems to me you shouldn't bother with expensive leather bags. They're a good status symbol, but it will break your heart to see them, or what's left of them, after a few trips with the airlines.

TIP

If you travel a lot and carry expensive clothes or other personal items, get in the habit of saving the purchase receipts at home. Then, if you have to make a loss claim on a bag, you can verify the high value of your lost clothing.

AVOIDING LOST BAGGAGE

If you do find yourself a victim of loss or damage, there are limits on the airline's liability, and the process of making a claim is slow and painstaking. Domestic baggage liability is up to a maximum of $750 per passenger, but such things as fragile items—how our instruments are categorized—are not covered at all. On international flights the maximum liability is approximately $9.07 per pound ($20 per kilo) for checked baggage and $400 maximum on unchecked (carry-ons). In order to make a claim you are required to itemize the articles in your baggage and the approximate value. Obviously, many types of items such as clothing and jewelry would be difficult to assess and you can expect some haggling from the company.

You can purchase additional insurance for a nominal fee, though few people seem to bother with this. The airline probably wouldn't accept liability for unusual baggage either. In fact, if you are traveling with a musical instrument, the airlines will frequently ask you to sign a waiver that automatically absolves them of any responsibility. It's a cheap move on their part, but there's not much you can do about it if they insist you sign before checking your instrument.

To help spare you the grief of bags lost or damaged, take all possible precautions. First, and this is required by the airlines, clearly label *everything*. Preferably use more than one label in case one gets torn off. Second, also put your name and address *inside* for further identification. A suggestion I recently heard is not to use your home address when labeling: instead use a manager's office or other business office. Apparently, there is an increasing problem with thieves who look at the baggage labels on departing luggage to get home addresses for burglary prospects.

Next, further mark your bags with some sort of identifying colored tape or ribbon to help avoid confusion with look-alikes. I once had a piece of luggage make a flight connection with no bag tag at all (it must have gotten torn off inadvertantly) simply because it had yellow tape strips that matched our other bags so the handlers knew where it was supposed to go.

When you check your baggage at the terminal, be certain that the correct destination tags are put on. If you're changing planes enroute, a multidestination tag will be used listing each flight you'll take. If you're flying direct, a single tag bearing the name of the destination city will be attached.

Finally, be at the baggage claim area when the luggage comes through. Some airport terminals have security checks that require your bag check stub be matched with the bag tag, but most have no security whatsoever for keeping strangers from picking up what's not theirs.

When you have to make a connection, be sure that you or your travel agent has allowed sufficient time for your baggage to change planes too.

You can do two things if you're worried about this: first, you can keep an eye on the loading of the plane you're transferring to and possibly see your bags being put on; second, you can ask the agent to call the baggage service department and make certain your bags get transferred. If your bags still fail to appear at your destination, don't panic immediately. In most cases the delayed baggage will find its way via the next available flight; nevertheless, you will be ahead of the game if you inquire at the baggage counter.

If your bag is definitely not on the flight, then the baggage service counter is the place for you. In the efforts to locate it for you, you may be asked to fill out a lost baggage form, and clerks *can* call the airport you departed from to begin tracing procedures. If your bag is still among the missing after a day or two, *then* you can start worrying, for the tracing process gets results so quickly that no word after a couple of days means it is really lost. *Because lost bags are a fairly common occurrence, don't be tempted to put your passport, money, valuable papers, carnet forms, jewelry, or any items of great importance in your checked luggage.*

Misplaced baggage during foreign travel is even harder to track down, what with language problems, customs, etc., although the procedures for inquiring and tracing are the same as in domestic situations. If it were my bag, I would call the airline's baggage service in each city along the route and *not* leave it entirely in the hands of the airport agent.

======================= TIP =======================

Oversized pieces or fragile items may be brought to a place near the baggage claim area instead of coming through the conveyor belt system with the rest of the luggage. If you are missing an unusual item, see if your errant article is being held in a separate place.

===

CANCELLATIONS AND DELAYS

If you are informed that your flight has been canceled or is delayed when you are in the airport, you may or may not get some help from the airline. If it is a cancellation, the company will customarily make a solid effort to get you on an alternate flight. If it's a delay, they might not be so helpful in switching you to another company. So you should check on availability of other flights yourself. Delayed flights have a way of getting further and further delayed as the usually optimistic airline gradually runs out of options to get it off the ground.

Having a back-up plan can save you from blowing an important date because of occasional last-minute surprises with the airlines. Try to pick a flight other than the last possible one to get you there in time, and make note of the flight number and time of the "last resort" flight. Then if you get scratched from your earlier flight, you can probably still make the engagement via the later flight.

TIP

It's better to have a long layover and know your instruments will arrive with you than to have a brief 20-to-30-minute connection time and arrive without your things. In foreign countries, 1 or 2 hours are required for luggage to change planes, particularly in some countries, so play it safe with longer connecting times if your instruments are checked as baggage.

OVERBOOKING

Using computer statistics to tell them the average number of no-shows on a particular route, the airlines customarily book more passengers than seats available in order to compensate for no-shows. Occasionally they misjudge.

The overbooking procedure for the airline is first to ask all the passengers if any will voluntarily agree to go on a later flight to solve the problem. Amazingly enough, some people do volunteer. (The airlines will often offer a cash payment, say, $50 to $100, to any passenger willing to take a later flight.) Next, the airline will try to deal with the extra passengers as best they can. If they can find an alternate flight or flights for the bumped passengers, one that arrives at their destination no later than two hours after their originally scheduled arrival (four hours later on U.S. to Canada flights), then the airline is absolved of any further responsibility.

If this is not possible and the only available flights are later than the two-hour grace period, then the airline must pay a compensation fee equal to the fare on the segment of the trip that was missed (from a minimum of $25 to a maximum of approximately $400). At the present there is some discussion about the possibility of the compensation being changed to double the ticket cost. If you are ever the victim of overbooking, be sure to ask about compensation.

In most cases the seats are handed out according to boarding cards. Once you've got a boarding card, you're pretty certain to have a seat. Obviously, my advice is to check in early and if necessary go to the gate to get your boarding card well before flight time.

Unfortunately, a few airlines issue boarding passes and seat assignments only at the gate and only about 30 to 40 minutes prior to flight time. Delta is one of the large airlines that functions this way, and sometimes United does. It causes a panic rush at the gate counter as people compete for passes and seating. Groups traveling together, families with children, and the elderly suffer particularly on crowded flights, often not getting to sit together and having to stand in long check-in lines. And if you're the last in line, you may find you're one of the overbooked who doesn't get a seat.

Certainly the system used by TWA, American, and others is best. People are given boarding passes and seat assignments as they arrive at the airport or even in advance when the reservations are made so that there's no last-minute panic or hassles. Hopefully, this eventually will be the system used by all the airlines.

The slickest move I ever saw in an overbooking was on a flight in Japan some years ago. The tour manager, Charles Bourgois from George Wein's company, realized after everyone was on board that there was one too few seats, so he ducked into the lavatory until the plane had taken off. When he emerged in midflight, the stewardess apologized for his inconvenience and offered him the jump seat in the galley. [I don't think an American airline would be too gracious about it, CAB (Civil Aeronautics Board) rules being rather sacrosanct, but it was well received in Japan.] I was truly impressed with Charlie's ingenuity in handling the situation.

TIP

If the counter lines are long and frantic, go to the public phones and call the airline reservation number. If there is space available on another flight you want, you have just booked yourself a reservation and bypassed some of the hassle.

AIRPORT SECURITY
Many changes have been made over the past few years in airport security. Baggage lockers are quickly disappearing from airport lobbies, and only European airports still offer checkrooms for temporary storage. Also in many cities air freight shipments are being held for an extra day for security reasons before they can be sent out.

(Presumably, the bomb will go off within 24 hours.) Personal security ranges from electronic scanning commonly used in the U.S. to total frisking by police officers in some foreign airports, which can add delays to boarding times. Unless you know the airport runs efficiently, allow some extra time for this very necessary inconvenience.

CROWDED AIR TERMINALS
This can be predicted in many larger airports during holiday periods, and just getting there can be more than difficult during bad weather. Consider such delays when booking reservations and try to avoid making connections in these large airports. But if you must use airports with reputations for delays, then allow extra time for getting there, checking-in, making connections, and security checks.

=== TIP ===

When there's an opportunity for changing planes in Indianapolis, St. Louis, or Kansas City instead of Chicago, by all means do so. Chicago's O'Hare can be a major scene of congestion when under stress. New York's Kennedy Airport is also a disaster a lot of the time.

Some larger airports require that you change terminal buildings with a bus or tram service in order to make connections. I have waited a half an hour or longer to get the bus in New York and at Newark Airport too. I always try for connections in cities where I can walk from one terminal area to another. It's a lifesaver when the connecting time is short.

SPECIAL TREATMENT
It is possible to get service and assistance above and beyond the usual by using tact and some show biz razzle-dazzle. For instance, large groups can be preboarded to make it easier for everyone, depending on the cooperation of the gate agent. Contacting the supervisor in advance is usually the best way to arrange VIP treatment for a known group.

Excess and oversized baggage can sometimes be passed through without problems by giving a call to the airline in advance to explain your particular needs. More than once I have avoided large excess baggage costs on international trips by informing the airline that a well-known American group is traveling with them and asking for their assistance when we check in at the airport the next day (even though they've probably never heard of us, they often cooperate and assume that they should know who we are).

A travel agent who deals extensively with an international airline can also have some influence through the airline's executives in arranging baggage allowance and special assistance. (It's supposed to be against the rules for the airline to allow excess baggage for nothing or for cut-rates; however, it happens all the time and it doesn't hurt to discreetly try. Sometimes all costs are waived and sometimes, just to observe form, you'll be charged a token amount.)

VIP lounges are fancy waiting areas where refreshments are sometimes provided as well as various additional services. The international airlines make them available to first class passengers and important figures, but in America the government decided that it was unfair to discriminate against tourist passengers. So the VIP lounges are available to both first class and tourist passengers providing you join the airline's VIP club, with yearly membership dues. To be covered by most of the major airlines, you have to join about half a dozen of them. Obviously this is the sort of thing that appeals mainly to business executives who usually have the membership costs covered by their company.

With international airlines, an advance request with the reservations agent will probably be enough to arrange an invitation wait in the VIP lounge until flight time.

MISCELLANEOUS AIRLINE INFORMATION
Some items are forbidden in your luggage: cigarette lighters, matches, fireworks, flammables, firearms.

Another good thing to know is that the very first row at the front of each section (first class and tourist) is called the bulkhead seat and there is little foot room there and no room for carry-on baggage. So if you have something with you, don't choose that row of seats. However, this first row is often preferred by people traveling with acoustic basses because no one in the row in front can lean their seat back on the instrument.

The flight insurance that you see offered in the lobbies of airports is supposedly no bargain. The rates charged are considered disproportionately high. So unless you have a strong premonition that this flight is your last, pass on it. A better bargain is the automatic $75,000 or so flight insurance you get whenever you charge your ticket on a major credit card. Or take out a travel accident policy for the whole year at more reasonable rates through the Airline Passengers Association (described later in this chapter), the Auto Club, or your insurance agent.

TIP

Small planes, often operated by so-called commuter airlines, have several negative characteristics. Besides the shortage of space for baggage, they have a less-than-comforting safety record, and schedules are not adhered to in many cases.

TYPES AND SIZES OF PLANES
First, a word or two about differences in planes. Almost everyone agrees that the 747 is the most comfortable and desirable plane available. It has plenty of room and an excellent safety record. The other jumbos—the DC-10 and the Airbus—are also roomy and comfortable. Some jumbo planes are operated with larger seats in tourist for the extra comfort of the passengers, such as those on Swissair (nine seats across instead of ten). For long international trips, 707s and DC-8s are more cramped and not nearly so desirable as the jumbos.

On short routes, the medium-sized jets—727, 737, DC-9, etc.—are all similar and comfortable, all things considered. Generally, it's on the long hauls that such things as your seat, foot room, walking-around room, etc., become a major factor.

Types and sizes of planes will matter to you if you carry any large pieces of equipment or any great quantity of general baggage. Large jets have a practically limitless capacity for quantities and sizes of baggage. However, prop planes and small jets have a limited space for baggage, and leaving behind large pieces or excess bags for later flights if a plane reaches its maximum load limit is a common occurrence. Remarkably, the passengers aren't always told about this until *after* they have arrived at their destination. You might find that you're there, but your instruments aren't and won't be until the next day—too late for the concert.

I generally try to avoid having to rely on small planes and make arrangements for equipment to go by some other means. Always ask your travel agent or airline representative to specify which kind of plane you will be using.

On my last venture on a commuter line, Aspen Airways in Colorado was hours late, the baggage didn't make it until a later flight, and they have a carry-on bag weight limit of 5 pounds!

I usually prefer going by car or through alternate cities to avoid potential problems.

DIFFERENCES IN U.S. AIRLINES
Supposedly all the airlines offer identical service when it comes to basics, and the main items are in fact regulated quite strictly by government agencies. There are differences in attitude and service, however, which become apparent to the frequent traveler. The differences are not uniform, of course, and you will occasionally get extra good service on an airline which is habitually slack and really pitiful service on an airline that is normally reliable. Here are some of my own personal observations based on my own experiences (these are my personal opinions):

American Airlines and TWA: These two airlines are popular with me and seem to be with most musicians I've talked with because their attitude toward the passengers is very positive, and they are flexible regarding excess or unusual baggage. I did hear about someone having trouble bringing a bass into the cabin on American recently.

United: This is the other very large company, and although it serves a lot of cities, I have always found their attitude a little less courteous. Several times I have even had hassles with them over baggage.

Braniff, Continental, Delta, Eastern, National, Northwest: These are large companies serving large regions of the country, and I have had problems with all these companies at one time or another, sometimes over baggage, sometimes with personal service. Eastern has improved considerably in the past few years; however, there was a time when I considered this airline to have the worst possible attitude toward passengers. I have had many problems with Delta and don't like their last-minute seat selection process which I described before, so I generally try to avoid them if I have a choice.

AirWest, Frontier, Piedmont, Republic, US Air, Others: These airlines are smaller, regional carriers and tend to operate smaller planes, with less service offered to the passenger. They are more often subject to crowded departure areas and less-than-adequate staff to handle large crowds. My all-time least favorite airline in this category is US Air which has repeatedly botched up trips for me over the years.

You may be mistreated or wronged in some way by an airline employee. Feel free to complain. You can speak to supervisors, and you can write to the company, which will always write back and apologize. Placating complainants is someone's full-time job. You may not get any real justice, but I do believe in speaking up when taken advantage of.

If it's a serious infraction of fairness or rules, you can complain to the appropriate agency—the Civil Aeronautics Board (CAB) for domestic service, the International Airline Transport Association (IATA) for international—and possibly get some stronger results.

FOREIGN AIRLINES

There are a few differences between domestic and international air travel of which the U.S. passenger should be aware. First, as mentioned earlier, international tickets are not as freely exchangable between different airlines as they are in the United States. Also, don't expect to appear at the ticket counter an hour before flight time and have your international ticket rewritten in time for the flight you want to catch. If the fare stays the same, then it may be rather quick, but if the ticket has to be recalculated or rerouted, the time might be long enough to make you think you could have walked. Ticket rewrites are best handled at an intown ticket office a day or two before flying. Frequently, you'll need to leave tickets for a day or two for rewriting.

There is also a practice of requiring the traveler to reconfirm ongoing reservations each time you arrive in a stopover city. If you don't reconfirm within 72 hours, your reservation may be canceled and the space sold to other customers. Europe is about evenly divided between countries which require you to reconfirm and those which don't. Consequently, it is a good idea to *always* confirm your next flight unless it happens to be within 24 hours (in which case the airline automatically holds your reservation). Reconfirming can also save you from last-minute surprises, such as a flight which may not be operating or an airline which is unexpectedly on strike (fairly frequent in Europe).

In the less technologically advanced countries airlines may not have computer systems to help with their booking and ticketing procedures. If you should happen to need a ticket change or confirmation in such circumstances, it will take a day or two, or possibly even longer, for communications to take place by cable or telex.

=== TIP ===

European flights are very rigid regarding carry-on baggage—only one piece per person. And sometimes, no electronic devices (tape recorders, amplifiers, to name a few) are allowed in the cabin for security reasons. Don't expect to get past this because they are very strict in many countries.

DIFFERENCES IN INTERNATIONAL AIRLINES

Pan Am and TWA: These are the two U.S. companies which handle the majority of the international flight business. (Northwest flies to Japan and American, Braniff, Delta, and Eastern fly to the Caribbean and Latin America as well as offer some flights to Europe.) I have always found that the service with the American companies is not nearly so nice as that with the foreign. Those long international flights give the airline a chance to provide a wide variety of services and circumstances.

Sabena and British Air: For what it's worth, I've had less than ideal experiences with Sabena and British Air this past year. Sabena had a terrible attitude toward the passengers on my flight. British Air has pathetic food, especially in first class. Also, British Air flights are often routed in and out of Heathrow Airport in London, one of the most likely in the world to be having a crisis. Strikes, fuel shortages, fog, overcrowding are all commonplace. I always hold my breath and keep my fingers crossed whenever I have to make connections at Heathrow.

Concorde: For those who might consider it, the Concorde offers service from New York and Washington to London and Paris in three hours less than the regular transatlantic flight. The arrivals in Europe are usually too late to make same-day connections to other cities, so you might not save so much time if you're going some place other than London or Paris. But Air France will provide a free luxury hotel room near the airport if you need to stay overnight for a connection the next day. Also, the Concorde is short on space: very cramped inside, with limited foot room and small space for carry-on baggage. Fares are a few hundred dollars above regular first class.

The big advantage with the Concorde is that you avoid jet lag. The conventional jet service from the U.S. east coast departs in the evening, flies through the night, and arrives the next morning in Europe. So in addition to the time change, you also lose an entire night's sleep while sitting up all night in the plane seat. The effects of jet lag are thus greatly worsened. With the Concorde, the travel is during daytime hours so that you arrive in time to go to bed. Your trip gets off to a better start.

PRIVATE CHARTER FLIGHTS

As extravagant as this might sound, it is actually worth considering sometimes. If your group consists of enough people, say, four or more, then the per passenger fare is often not much more than the commercial fare. The advantages are being able to travel on your own schedule and using a small airport that may be less congested and closer to your destination. One disadvantage is that luggage space is very limited on a small plane, so forget it if you have a lot of instruments or any unusually large ones.

Another consideration might be comfort. Since small planes are both cramped and bouncy, the squeamish might prefer a large jet. Borderline weather conditions will keep the small planes from flying too, when the large ones still operate.

Sometimes a sudden change in plans will mean trying to locate a private charter flight on short notice in order to get to a performance. This can often be done in a few hours; however, it is better to plan ahead and make advance arrangements if time permits.

OFFICIAL AIRLINE GUIDE (OAG)

The OAG is used by airline reservation clerks and travel agents to locate available flights and connections offered by all the airlines.

The book is as thick as a major city telephone book and is updated with the latest schedules every two weeks. If you are curious about some future travel you are planning, a look in the OAG will tell you flight times, connection cities, type of aircraft, meal services, number of stops, etc. You can frequently find a copy of the OAG in an airplane's magazine rack for browsing while in flight (although as an economy gesture, some airlines are no longer providing them on planes).

If you travel by air a considerable amount, having your own OAG delivered by mail is worth the subscription price. It is available in several forms. The full version updated every two weeks costs $119.64 per year plus postage, as of this year, and a ground transportation service book comes gratis. The full version updated once a month costs $85.80 plus postage each year. There is also a pocket-size version listing the most popular flights between cities, but not all the possibilities, which is updated each month and costs $38.92 plus postage. (see Appendix C for ordering and more complete information on this and other guides.)

APA (AIRLINE PASSENGERS ASSOCIATION)

The APA could come in handy for the frequent air traveler. You can become a member for a small yearly fee which entitles you to a newsletter of recent changes and tips on dealing with the airlines, discounts at many hotels and rental car agencies, plus various low-cost group insurance plans. They also have a baggage tracing system (they will provide special baggage stickers for all your luggage) and even a toll-free number for weather updates for any major city in the world. In addition, the APA has considerable leverage when it comes to helping their members straighten out misunderstandings with the airlines.

===**TIP**===

APA's 30 percent discount (in most cases) on car rentals represents a major savings for most travelers and more than pays for the yearly membership. (See Appendix C for the APA's address.)

TRAINS

Train travel is enjoying a partial recovery in the U.S. although it still is not competitive with air or highway travel. Being transported in comfort, such as in a private room or sleeping compartment, is expensive and the standards of service and equipment vary widely from new and adequate to old and irritating. And U.S. trains are simply not on time. However in some European countries and Japan, train service is a reliable, relaxing, and reasonable way to travel—sometimes more convenient than flying. (See Foreign Trains later in this section.)

RESERVATIONS
As with airlines, a phone call is the way to reserve space on a train. Just call Amtrak in the U.S. and the local rail office in European cities. However, not all seating on trains is reserved, so if you are travelling a short distance or simply going as a coach passenger, there may be no reservations required. Special sleeping accommodations, compartments, and roomettes always need reservations in advance.

TIP

At least on foreign trains, it is usually possible to stow bulky baggage items at the ends of the train or along the side in the aisle if you don't have room for everything at your seat. Also I have sometimes bought extra seats in a compartment in Europe to have room for the equipment and luggage.

BAGGAGE
The preferred approach to carrying baggage on trains is to take your luggage to your seat area and stow it in the rack overhead or nearby. The other option is to check it at the station. If you find this necessary, it does make your arrangements slightly more complicated. Unless the train is terminating at your destination, the ordinary waiting time in a station is *but a few minutes,* so be ready to disembark without delay.

Porters are in extremely short supply these days, but can be found to assist with baggage. The usual tipping applies: about 50¢ to $1 per bag.

TICKET PURCHASES

For the most part, purchases are made in advance at train booking offices or through travel agents. Checks are acceptable generally with good identification, but this is nothing to bank on, and some credit cards are accepted.

=== TIP ===

Don't count on train travel in Europe if you carry a ton of equipment. It is only practical for light travelers.

FOREIGN TRAINS

Trains in Europe and Japan offer different classes of service. First class is very comfortable, with large spacious seating. Second is not much different. Most travelers consider it equally comfortable and it is, of course, less expensive. Third class, when offered, is quite Spartan and extremely inexpensive.

When crossing a border, passports and identification will be checked on board by customs officials in the vicinity of the border. Any baggage checked in the baggage car might be detached from the train and kept for customs inspection, to be sent on with the next through train. This can be a terrible inconvenience, obviously. I became aware of this the hard way in Italy a few years ago. Two other bands and my group were stuck waiting in a nearly freezing Milan train terminal for five hours while our baggage car—which we had watched with alarm being uncoupled at the Swiss-Italian border—went through inspection there. In the meantime, we took turns watching our other luggage and trying to find ways to keep warm, while waiting for the next train to bring it to Milan.

In Europe I have found the train service a direct reflection of how the country generally operates. The trains in Switzerland, Germany, and Scandinavia are extremely nice and punctual, for instance, and the ones in Italy, Spain, Yugoslavia, for instance, are less new and often run late.

EURAIL PASSES

One of the great travel bargains anywhere, the ticket must be purchased *outside* Europe and entitles you to travel on any and all trains in Europe with few exceptions. The travel is first class for set periods of time: there is a two-week pass, a month-long pass, and so on. If you have an extensive itinerary, it can represent a considerable savings over air fares or car rentals.

If you anticipate a lot of train travel in Europe, you might want to obtain the Eurail Guide, listing all the train schedules. (See Appendix C for the address for Eurail Guide information.) Your travel agent also has a guide with which to explain the various choices and can arrange the purchase of a pass for you.

BUS

CHARTERING A BUS

This can be very practical since a bus almost always offers plenty of room for instruments and friends. Particularly in Europe, buses for hire come in small, medium, and large sizes complete with driver. Any travel agent can charter a bus for you or a bus company can be called directly. In Europe even the hotel desk can put you in touch with a reputable company.

Rates are surprisingly reasonable and the prevailing service, friendly and efficient. It is generally an accepted practice to pay the lodging expenses and possibly the meals too for a driver if overnight stays are involved. Also a tip for the driver is customary—something like $5 to $20 per day depending on the circumstances, namely, whether there are any marathon-length drives required or if the driver helps with loading and unloading of the equipment.

TRAVELING BY BUS

The only advantages of going by commercial bus which come to mind are that fares are low and express service between major cities isn't too uncomfortable.

RENTAL CARS

There is a wide choice in picking a rental company. Everyone knows about the three major ones—Hertz, Avis, and National, of course—but recent legislation giving the smaller companies access to airport areas has made this business much more competitive. And even locally operated rental companies are getting into the business and offering some of the best bargains.

THE BIG THREE

These present the best service, the newest vehicles, and the most convenient locations. Naturally their rates are higher, but their convenience and reliability often make this worthwhile. For instance, if you need to rent a particular car type, such as a station wagon, one of the big three companies is more likely to have one available and guaranteed, even in out-of-the-way places. Many large city majors have vans for rental too. Suburban carryall vans and "blazers" are listed now, but these are most likely to be found in Western cities where four-wheel drive is in demand.

If you can show some working affiliation with a large organization (record company, university, etc.), the major companies offer a 10 to 20 percent business discount (except on discount or special rentals) which makes their prices competitive with the less expensive companies. Airline Passengers Association and AAA (Auto Association of America) members qualify for a 30 percent discount. These substantial discounts make the rates of the major companies competitive with the smaller companies. And the small cost of membership in either of these worthwhile organizations becomes a major bargain if you do much auto renting. The majors also offer their own credit cards and preregistration service. You can use any nationally recognized credit card, of course, but with the car company's own card you may be entitled to a discount, the bill will be sent to you directly instead of being added to the other items on your credit card account, and clerks can fill out your rental contract in advance, speeding pick-up time. (You may experience major delays in picking up rental cars during rush periods in large city airports. Waits of thirty minutes to an hour are not uncommon.)

LOWER-PRICED NATIONAL FIRMS

Companies such as Ajax, Budget, Dollar-a-Day, Thrifty, etc., have outlets nationwide at most major airports and offer lower rates. They also have smaller discounts, if any, fewer choices of vehicles available, and pick-up locations farther from the terminals. Also road service in case of breakdown tends to be less available than with the major chains. But it never hurts to check them out. For certain rental situations, it might be cheaper to deal with one of these.

LOCALLY OWNED FIRMS

These rental companies, sometimes part of an auto dealership or a department store chain, are definitely the cheapest way to go but have their own limitations. There usually aren't pick-up areas at the airports, and they don't offer autos for drop-off in other cities. However, long-term rentals of a month or so are definitely most economical from one of these outfits, and if you are looking for a van, you might have to go to one of these local companies if the airport locations don't have any available.

Another alternative in the car rental field is to rent an elderly used car. I first tried this in 1965 in Las Vegas when I rented a decade-old Pontiac from a man who worked out of a parking lot behind a hotel. There was no paperwork and he was very loose—undoubtedly not properly insured. Still, it was just twenty-five dollars a week for a perfectly driveable car.

Nowadays there are fully certified rental companies dealing in old cars. One that advertises nationally is Rent-A-Wreck, whose national number is (800) 228-5000.

ONE-WAY TRAVEL

The delights of "Rent it here, leave it there" car rentals are dampened in many circumstances by an extra charge for drop-off and by the unavailability of unlimited mileage rates. But it may be practical for you if your travel itinerary requires it.

TIP

Drop-offs in other cities are not permitted with certain types of rentals—station wagons, vans, specialty cars, for instance. So don't count on it without checking first. Also the major companies are more equipped to handle this type of rental than others.

REQUIREMENTS

The requirements for renting a car are increasingly strict and it is now commonly assumed that a credit card is a necessity for this. You can still rent from some outlets with a cash deposit, providing you have good credit references and fill out the necessary information forms in advance for the company's approval. A travel agent might also be able to help make the arrangements if you don't have a credit card.

The age requirements start at eighteen if you have an approved credit card and twenty-one otherwise. Twenty-five is the minimum age for renting with a cash deposit from some companies, and renting special vehicles such as vans sometimes requires at least age twenty-five. Foreign rentals are at least twenty-one and often twenty-five. Of course, a valid driver's license is required.

=== TIP ===

Any person who will be driving the car must have his or her name and driver's license listed on the rental contract in order to be properly insured. A lot is risked when a car is driven by an uninsured driver.

RATES

Most companies propose two different rate plans to choose from. The standard is so much charged per day, week, or month plus so much per mile. This is the best bet for short-term rentals with a low number of miles to be driven. For longer trips there is the other option of paying a set rate per day, with unlimited mileage at no charge, and returning the car to the city of rental. No special discounts are available on unlimited mileage rentals, however. Most companies will compute the bill whichever way is the most economical for the customer. But inquire about it before you rent. Again, some companies don't offer unlimited mileage with certain vehicles such as station wagons and vans, and the rules may vary from one city or state to another. The customer always pays for the gas and oil.

As you are aware, rates vary from city to city, and special package deals, weekend rates, and the like proliferate. The ground transportation guide that comes with the Official Airline Guide will help tell you which companies serve each city and what models they carry. Rates must be determined by calling the local office of each company. For expensive rentals, it can really pay to shop around for the best deal.

Definitely reserve early if you need a specialty car such as a wagon or a van. Even a month or more in advance is suggested since they are often in big demand and short supply.

If you need major repairs, you should call the renting company for instructions and their authorization to get the work done. They will, of course, pay for the costs. If you can't afford the time to wait for service work, then it's a stickier situation. There's a good chance of getting a substitute car if you're still in the local area where you rented it. If you're in another city, it might mean dropping off the ailing car and renting another, thereby incurring drop-off charges and losing corporate discounts or possible discounts for unlimited mileage. The major companies are definitely more cooperative about repair and breakdown situations.

It doesn't hurt to check the condition of the car, tires, and spare tire when you pick up the auto. My brother once rented a car from Avis in France with bald tires and a flat spare. The police stopped him en route and made him go purchase a completely new set of tires. The company paid the cost, of course, but the inconvenience wasn't welcome.

===TIP===

If you already have a valid state driver's license, an international driver's license is available without taking any tests. The international licenses are issued by the AAA. Just contact your nearest local office for information on what to do.

Beware of driving in Mexico. There are many horror stories of people getting into extended litigation or being jailed after routine auto accidents. You're definitely taking some risks driving in this country.

RESERVATIONS AND VEHICLE SIZE

The quick pick-up and reservation service that the major companies offer will save you five or ten minutes but won't make up for the wrong-sized car. Ask about the actual size car you hope to rent. Intermediate car models are now often called "full-sized" by the rental companies, but four or five passengers, instruments, and baggage will be a tight squeeze. Large, four-door sedans are now often classified as "luxury" size and are not always available, as is true of station wagons. Even station wagons can turn out to be little compact wagons and still be called full-sized by the company. (I don't understand how the car rental companies can get away with this, but they certainly do.)

The rental van which costs approximately the same as a station wagon in most locations is still a bargain. And there's no problem about plenty of space either. It's a good idea to insist on a confirmation when you make the reservation, and be sure to reserve specialty vehicles (wagons, vans) well in advance. And remember with vans and wagons no drop-offs in other cities are available.

INSURANCE
Basic accident insurance is automatically sold to you or included in the rental price, but two additional coverages are also offered. The basic insurance on the car is usually $500 deductible collision insurance. The company will offer you a collision damage waiver so that you can avoid having to pay the first $500 in an accident. For this you pay about $5 per day. This means you will have to have an accident every 100 rental days in order to break even. So unless you're accident prone, it doesn't really make sense. Plus the rate they're charging is considerably overpriced, as insurance rates go.

The other insurance is called Personal Accident Insurance. This is really misleading. It's mostly life insurance. The small print says that the insurance pays something like $1,500 of the medical costs in an accident (a mere pittance by the standard's of today's medical expenses) and from $150,000 to $200,000 in case of death in an accident of the individual renting the car. In short, this is a life insurance policy with a trivial medical benefit thrown in. If you already have health insurance, then you would be better off buying a less expensive travel accident insurance policy each year instead of paying the extra $5 per day or more for this coverage.

Important note: Don't forget that car rental companies will probably hold you liable in an accident if there is proof of illegalities such as an underage or unauthorized driver, illegal substances in the car, intoxication, or even an opened bottle of alcoholic beverage in the car (a crime in most states), leaving you totally responsible for what could be hundreds of thousands of dollars in damages and injury claims. Don't take this lightly as a major disaster of this kind could totally change your life. (See Auto Insurance in Chapter 6 for further discussion.)

Also, you are responsible for all parking tickets received while you rent a car, and they will track you down to collect.

FOREIGN RENTALS

These are comparable with the U.S. companies in form, except that the rental fees are considerably higher. All the major and near-major companies are represented in Europe and Japan. In Europe each car carries an insurance registration card, the so-called green card, which may be inspected when you cross borders. An ordinary U.S. driver's license is generally accepted all over Europe and Japan. However, technically, East Germany and perhaps the other Eastern Bloc countries require an international driver's license.

RENTAL TRUCKS AND TRAILERS

Most of the same conditions for car rentals apply to renting anything from a van to a truck, except that age and credit prerequisites may be more strict. You may not be able to pay for truck or trailer rentals with a credit card, though some places will accept Mastercharge or Visa. The minimum age limit on truck rentals is usually at least twenty-five, and higher cash deposits are often required for truck rentals. Vans are often available for pick-up and drop-off at airports, though larger trucks are not. And drop-off in other cities is quite available.

Make sure you are qualified to drive a large truck if you plan to rent one. They have a higher accident rate and certain restrictions such as height, and certain streets and roads may be off-limits. This also applies to trailers in many cases. The rule of thumb on vans and small trucks is that a truck with windows all around is usually not considered a commercial vehicle unless it has a commercial license plate. A truck enclosed with no windows on the sides and back is usually always considered a commercial truck and is forbidden on many parkways, boulevards, downtown streets, etc. New York City is particularly restrictive in this regard, so take it into consideration if you're going to be traveling there.

Renting a trailer in a variety of sizes and shapes is easy and reasonably priced as a rule. But before you can show your taillights to the company man, a deposit equal to the anticipated rental price plus $10 to $20 is usually required. Sometimes more. Advance reservations are a good policy in large cities and during busy seasons and may necessarily require a small deposit. Warning: It is much less expensive to return the truck or trailer in the same city it was rented in than to drop it off in a different city. The most important thing to remember is that you *must* have a suitable trailer hitch and a suitable bumper—an item not built into newer or small cars—in order not to leave your precious belongings *and* the trailer on the median strip as you round your first curve. Although the renting company will help you with the following, be prepared to know about and deal with carefully balanced loading, light hookups, locks, possible blown fuses, and heavy-duty turn-signal flashers. You may have to rent or have installed a hitch, light connectors, exterior mirrors, etc.

TAXIS AND LIMOUSINES

TAXIS

In the United States taxis are rather expensive except for short distances or with a group of people. They are easy to locate on the streets in large cities (except when you desperately need one) but must be called in smaller cities and towns. In foreign cities hotel clerks or doormen will summon cabs, but the hotel will have to pay the taxidriver a "disappointment fee" if you duck out.

Tipping is around 20 to 25 percent in the U.S. and England; however, in Europe and Japan, little or no tipping is done unless you have a considerable amount of baggage. An offer to make it worth the cabbie's while may help you, but there is limited baggage space in foreign-made cabs and they are legally restricted to a maximum of four passengers, with no exceptions.

LIMOUSINE SERVICE

This is popular with many musicians. A car and driver are available for rental in medium and larger cities, as are chauffer-driven vans for luggage and equipment. The rates might be comparable with taxi fares depending on your needs. They are available by the hour or the day and are often more convenient than relying on taxis or dealing with parking problems with rental cars.

Tipping of limo drivers is customary, particularly if the driver deals with a lot of baggage or provides other forms of assistance. Limo service can be paid by cash or credit cards or billed to your place of business.

LEASING

This is an increasingly popular type of car ownership. Most car dealers have auto leasing available, while rental car companies also lease cars and might have competitive leasing rates. If you drive as much as 20,000 to 30,000 miles a year, you may find that it costs less or at least the same to lease instead of buying a car through the usual installment plan. A big plus is avoiding that inevitable trading of cars every few years, which most of us find traumatic at best. Leasing primarily offers convenience, readily determined tax deductions, and not having to tie up money in a down payment.

A typical lease involves a one- or two-month advance deposit or perhaps a small damage deposit. Some arrangements are closed-ended, which stipulate a set number of years after which the car must be returned. Others are open-ended, with a provision that after the lease is up, the car is sold, and depending on the price it brings, you may have to pay extra or get a refund to equal the estimated value of the vehicle at the time of resale. It pays to shop around, obviously, since rates do vary. Some companies that advertise incredibly low rates actually end up tacking on so many extra charges that it isn't cheap at all. Better to deal with a company that is at least straightforward in its offers.

Most leases do not include maintenance and the lease customer is expected to pay for the upkeep of the car. You can get full maintenance leases at much higher cost, of course, but it is only practical if you expect to keep the car always in the vicinity of the dealer so he can make the repairs. If you do much out-of-town travel, then it wouldn't be a good idea.

BEING PREPARED

It is sensible to equip your car with the following: road atlas, Disto-Map (for estimating mileages between cities), jumper cables, spare lamp bulbs, spare fuses, spare alternator belt, small tool assortment, flashlight, length of wire, coat hanger wire, couple of rags, and a small shovel and windshield scraper for winter driving.

MAPS AND GUIDES

For planning tours by car or plane, two invaluable aids are a Rand McNally Road Atlas and a Disto-Map, which are available at bookstores and some filling stations. Best routes, distances, and travel times can be easily planned in advance with these handy guides.

In Europe, the Falkplan Company offers colorful and complete maps of all European countries and all major cities. These can be bought at some U.S. bookstores, such as Brentano's in the East, or at European airports and gas stations. In addition, there is a hard-cover book published by Shell Oil in Germany, called the *Grosse Shell*

Atlas, that is considered the road traveler's bible in Europe. This atlas has maps of every European country in great detail and indexes of the cities, plus endless miscellaneous information such as ferry crossing details and local traffic laws.

For train travel in Europe, there is a guide for advance planning too. If you are entraining with or without a Eurailpass, take advantage of the Eurail Guide. (See Appendix C for address.)

The Michelin guidebooks are excellent for European countries for information on hotels and restaurants, and they include maps of most major cities. In England, the Egon Ronay Hotel Guide is the most popular. I have personally improved my travel plans on numerous occasions because I had the proper book to refer to for details on hotels, travel routes, special circumstances, and so on in areas with which I was not too familiar. (See Appendix C for list of these useful books and addresses.)

AUTO CLUBS

The main functions of these organizations, such as the Automobile Association of America (AAA) and similar clubs operated by some of the major oil companies, are to provide call-in information on road conditions and weather, towing service, and a battery boost if you're stuck. The only limitation is that the famous free tow is only to the nearest garage and not to your particular choice of repair place or dealer—for that it's extra. The yearly fee isn't expensive, so for someone who does considerable driving, joining could ward off problems of grand potential.

In addition, the AAA offers various group insurance plans for travel insurance, baggage insurance, and trip insurance. And they offer their members the same 30 percent group discount on major car rentals as the Airline Passengers Association.

An additional service they provide, though you don't have to be a member, is the issuance of international driver's licenses. There is no test involved; it's just a registration and an accepted international license with your photograph on it. (See Appendix C for the AAA's national address.)

CHAPTER 2

GETTING THE EQUIPMENT THERE

Equipment needs vary from one group to the next. Some musicians are lucky enough to be able to take along their instruments simply as personal baggage, while others face the endless work and juggling act of moving a ton or more of equipment. These maneuvers necessarily mean some sort of shipment and its inherent and ongoing problems.

CHOOSING CASES AND CONTAINERS

Selecting cases for equipment often results in a trade-off of conveniences. The strongest and most well-made, such as the famous Anvil brand and similar imitations, offers virtually damageproof service and protection. These are custom made, fiberglass and aluminum in construction with foam padding, and reinforced throughout. A band completely outfitted with these cases is ready to travel anywhere, under any conditions, but it will have thousands of dollars invested in cases and a moving job fit for the Mayflower Company. Major music stores and dealers found in the Yellow Pages can equip you with these highly esteemed containers.

The alternative is to choose the lighter-weight fiberboard cases. These containers are more moderately priced and lighter weight, and they don't add much to the dimensions of the instruments. The degree of protection is more suitable for drums than for something both heavy and delicate such as amplifiers. Limited life span due to constant minor damage (handles torn off, holes gouged, corners knocked off) eventually renders these cases too broken up to continue.

TIP

Reinforcing handles and varnishing overall will add miles to the life of fiberboard cases. Several coats of varnish forestalls warping caused by humidity and helps prevent gouges and breaks.

Improvisation: This is probably better received on the stage than on the road. Accordingly, don't expect air freight to accept your homemade case which is in reality a handleless suitcase with a rope tied around it or, worse, a slipshod box with exposed nails and hazardous corners. Shipping companies won't take anything too easily damaged by travel or dangerous to their workers.

SHIPPING AS EXCESS BAGGAGE

This option will be eliminated if you have too many oversized cases—or just too many—and will force you to ship via freight. When traveling internationally the high cost of excess might be prohibitive, although a tight schedule of performances and the delays of shipping and customs procedures could make it necessary. Always go early when your baggage limitations are in doubt and you will find much more cooperation and operating room. (See Checking in Your Baggage in Chapter 1.)

Excess baggage charges are computed, in both the U.S. and foreign airports, at the ticket counter, and that is where in the U.S. a ticket is written for the excess and stapled to your personal ticket. You can pay cash, check, or credit card. In foreign countries there is a separate counter or cashier's window where you actually pay for the charge and collect your boarding pass.

In foreign travel the big advantage to shipping as excess baggage, despite the cost, as opposed to air freight shipping, is that you can avoid monumental customs hassles by having it with you. I once watched a band from Chicago send their instruments as air freight instead of as checked baggage from Helsinki to Rome, and customs being what they are, I heard months later that they were *still* trying to find out what happened to their instruments. Certain countries have unreliable customs procedures, particularly France, Italy, Portugal, Spain, and Yugoslavia. The most timely and efficient are Scandinavia, Great Britain, Germany, Switzerland, and Austria. *Customs offices throughout the world are only open during business hours Monday through Friday (and usually closed for the lunch hour)*, so don't ever entertain the hope of claiming a freight shipment over the weekend if customs clearance is necessary. (See Customs Brokers later in this Chapter for more information on this.)

AIR FREIGHT

This is the most common method of shipping instruments and equipment. The least expensive approach to this is to take your paraphernalia directly to the freight terminal of the airline and claim it at the other end, thus avoiding local pickup and delivery charges. The time required for the shipping itself is a day or two under good conditions to a week or more during holidays and the never-completely-unexpected strike. Regulations on size allow virtually all instruments; however, a shoddy case improperly packed could possibly be refused.

The majority of a shipping company's business is done with large companies; consequently, the help an individual can expect varies. Often you are left cooling your heels in a waiting room or jockeying with truck drivers for attention. Generally the larger the airport, the less friendly the service and the more delay.

At weigh-in, the agent in customer service will write up an airway bill describing the equipment, its value, and beginning and end point addresses. It is very wise to have address tags attached in advance giving the sender's name and address as well as the receiver's in order to promote any rapport you may be able to establish with customer service. They don't usually provide labels for each case and expect you to have it labeled in advance.

Rates: These are steadily increasing, but shipping by air is still a reasonable way to get it there. The costs are computed by weight, with the one exception of a piece occupying a large amount of space but having very little weight. Several times I have had agents compute by both the per pound method and the cubic foot method to arrive at the *highest* rate.

For transatlantic shipping (U.S. to Europe, but not Europe to U.S.), there is a bargain flat rate for musical instruments that you might want to take advantage of that applies up to 200 Kilograms (440 pounds). Rates change constantly, but at present this flat rate tariff is in the vicinity of $350 for 200 kilos. Consult your airline, of course.

Payment: Air freight can be sent collect or prepaid. Some foreign shipments must be prepaid, but most often you can pay when you pick up. If you pay by check, the shipping company has the option to wait until the check clears—a common occurrence when shipping in foreign countries. Credit cards may be accepted too, but could be troublesome. Cash is handiest.

Transfers Between Airplanes: All airlines have air freight service and all have established rates. If you are transferring between planes domestically, no delay need be expected; however, the transfer time in a foreign airport, such as London, is a minimum of one day to as much as one week.

Avoid these connecting flight delays by taking the airline that has direct service to your destination. When searching for direct service, ask the agent point blank if any company *does* fly direct—he or she may not always volunteer the information without prompting.

Pickup: You can do this at the airline's freight terminal, which in large airports is located on the fringes and in smaller airports near the center of the terminal building itself. You can present your copy of the airway bill, if you have one, or simply offer the name designated as the receiver. Sometimes identification is requested, but most often you just pay up if it's collect or show that payment has been made. The airline customarily notifies you by phone or mail that shipments have arrived and storage fee charges will start after five business days.

Loss or Damage: The freight airbill lists both the value of the shipment itself and any extra insurance fee you might have had to pay if the value is unusually high as with musical instruments. A damage claim is realistic if the damage is clearly visible and can be shown immediately to the agent for verification. It is best to refuse to accept shipment until they have acknowledged responsibility for any damage.

Ironically, it is standard practice to be asked to sign a release form stating that the items have been received in good condition *before* seeing them. Better check the contents and the cases while you are still in the airport so that you can report any damage immediately—thereby establishing a claim on the spot. Airline companies are infamous for their skill at discouraging baggage damage claims so be prepared to be diligent in following through with any claims.

If they lose your shipment entirely, be prepared to wait for a while to see if it turns up somewhere. Then, if it doesn't, file a claim for the value of the equipment less depreciation. Any sales receipt or proof of value you might have would be helpful. In the only experience I have had with this, TWA paid in full with minimal hassle. (I don't know if this was good luck or not.)

Security: Sometimes freight shipments of personal items from individuals are held for 24 hours for security reasons. Locking the cases of expensive equipment to prevent tampering is a good idea, but don't send locked cases through customs by way of a broker who will need to open them for customs inspection (see Customs Broker later in Chapter).

FREIGHT FORWARDERS
Firms such as Emory, Wings & Wheels, etc., take the work out of freighting for you by picking up and delivering to your door, selecting the best airline routing, dealing directly with the airlines, and seeing to all details. You can minimize their fee by taking your shipment to their terminal office, thereby saving local pickup and delivery fees, but when you have a pile of equipment and no ground transport, one of these door-to-door companies is worth the cost. They are very reliable, I have found.

FOREIGN RAILWAY FREIGHT
In Europe or Japan this is dependable and quick. At-the-door pickup and delivey can be arranged for an extra fee, or you can simply go to a city's nearest large train station. Just be sure to allow at least an extra day if the shipment crosses an international border, and watch out for delays in customs from some countries.

TRUCKING
This is the cheapest way to go—although sometimes it is quick (a few days) and sometimes slow (a few months). You can take your shipment to the truck terminal, saving local pickup charges, or have them come to you. Check your Yellow Pages for a great variety of companies to choose from.

FREIGHT AND CUSTOMS
Freight shipments crossing international borders must go through customs only at the final destination. After settling the cost of shipping with the airline agent, you will be directed to a customs agent who will decide if you owe duty on anything in the shipment.

If you are traveling on tour you are not charged duty passing through, but many countries insist on having you register your instruments, especially if you have many. This international document of registration is called a "carnet" (pronounced kar-nay). (Detailed instructions on use are given in Chapter 5.)

If you are returning to the U.S. with a freight shipment, the customs official will want to know if anything is being imported. This is usually a matter of verifying that the instruments were made in the United States: brand names and serial numbers looked at, newness checked, etc. If it is of foreign manufacture, it is best to register it at a customs office *before* leaving the country to save returning to a hassle. Few questions are asked if the instrument and its case are clearly in used condition and were made in the U.S.

CUSTOMS BROKERS

These are commonly used if an international shipment needs to go to a destination with no customs facility. For a small fee a broker will see your equipment through a main customs terminal, taking care of all paperwork and usually corresponding with you through the mail.

Sometimes shipments of high value will require the use of a customs broker. This is definitely true for commercial shipments (recordings or new equipment) in excess of $500 that are entering the U.S.

CHAPTER 3

WHERE TO STAY

CHOOSING A HOTEL

Your choice of where you want to stay is a personal thing, of course. No judgments can be made except regarding convenience to the traveler. And the greatest convenience to come along in years is the advent of chain hotels and motels. At last there are certain consistent standards and reliable reservations. These chains, such as Holiday Inn, Howard Johnson's, Ramada Inn, Master Host, Quality Inn, Downtowner, and Travelodge, offer up-to-date, free directories with full descriptions of facilities, maps showing locations, and price lists. In addition, reservations can be made through the toll-free, computerized reservation system each chain has in operation. Regular travelers collect these directories as they go or order them by phone for later tour planning. The popular chains offer neither the lowest prices nor the most opulent accommodations in town, but for the one-night stop in a strange town they are usually the safest bet.

The *Travel Planner* from Reuben H. Donnelly (publisher of the Official Airline Guide) is a good reference for hotels. Besides offering a range of hotels in various prices in each city, it has a great deal of extra information (see Appendix C for details). The big advantage is that every little burg in the U.S. is listed so if the major hotel chains aren't represented there, you'll have a reliable source to consult. Also when a promoter suggests a hotel, you can check on its rating and prices in the book to see if it seems suitable for you. Sometimes promoters recommend overpriced places and sometimes they suggest fleabags, thinking you'll want to save every penny, so it's good to check on any hotel you're not familiar with.

TIP

The prices listed in the Travel Planner *are woefully out of date and will probably always be since hotel rates go up constantly. Assume that most rates will in actuality be as much as one-third more expensive than those listed.*

Between the "big two"—Holiday Inn and Howard Johnson's Motor Lodge—I have found Holiday Inns consistently better in service and cleanliness, although I've had some less-than-happy moments with them. While HoJo restaurants do often have 24-hour service as a plus, the motels usually don't have room service, which you may want. And there's the old joke about the ice cream coming in 28 flavors and the food coming in one, which definitely rings true. Of course, the same can frequently be said of Holiday Inn food.

Hotels and motels can be booked through your travel agent, but because the chains are less likely to give their lowest rates or entertainer discounts when they have to hand out commissions to the agent, you might do better if you make reservations yourself. The exception on discounts would be an agent-booked package plan. With the nationwide toll-free reservation numbers which the major chains have, it's quite easy to do it yourself if you have the little directories that they supply.

===== TIP =====

Many hotels/motels list their lowest priced rooms in the directories and brochures, and you will more often than not find that the least expensive rooms won't be available. Frequently the hotel has just a few inexpensive rooms, which are always booked, and only larger, double-type rooms at higher prices will be available.

I have found Holiday Inns to be the most straight-forward about pricing. It's always exactly as listed in their directory, although they frequently don't have one-bed rooms available (usually a few dollars less than two-bed rooms).

Some chains won't list prices in their directory or only give a vague reference such as $35 to $50, so you can't really tell without calling them yourself. This is another factor tending to recommend Holiday Inns.

SOME FACTORS TO CONSIDER

Standards of Quality: These are again a personal choice and range from spartan to sinfully luxurious. If you need either the best in town—gourmet all the way—or the cheapest possible, then your best bet is to contact someone locally, such as the promoter, for his advice, since neither of these two extremes is advertised much.

Access to Performance: Many performance centers in large cities and universities have hotels in the complex or next door, which make for great convenience, of course, although prices are sometimes high. Since many of these have special rates for performers, inquire through your local promoter.

=== TIP ===

When planning to use an airport hotel in a location you're not familiar with, purposely choose one that is located at least a few blocks away from the airport to ensure that the noise won't be too bad.

Access to Airports: If you are flying in or out, this is a consideration, especially if you have an early morning flight or you have to travel to the airport in the rush hour. As for airport hotels, they range from excellent to poor depending largely on airplane noise. Amazingly, some are so noisy you think that you are sleeping on the runway, while others are so well soundproofed that you never hear anything from outside. Ask the hotel clerk or the promoter if the hotel you are interested in is insulated or at least located a few blocks away from the terminal. By the way, the distance to the gig and the resulting taxi expenses should be taken into account when considering an airport hotel. These hotels almost always offer free courtesy transportation to and from the airport, but their schedules may be as infrequent as once an hour.

=== TIP ===

The Travel Planner *very handily lists separately some hotels near major airports so that you can find them when needed. When you use the courtesy transportation to or from the airport, you may need to tip the driver, particularly if it is one of the hotel bellhops.*

Access to Eating and Shopping: This is a small point, perhaps, but some hotels and motels are located in incredibly desolate areas, which would be inconvenient for lengthy stopovers. Also musicians are generally grateful to find food service available at odd hours and are particularly unhappy with hotel restaurants that close off and on through the day. When you're making the reservations, check on room service too, if that means a lot to you. It's an amenity that is slowly dying out, but there is still some range of service, from full menus in some places to styrofoam-packaged sandwiches in others.

TIP

As mentioned before, one major advantage of Howard Johnson's Motor Lodges is their 24-hour restaurant service. Also many LaQuinta Motor Inns seem to be located near 24-hour Denny's restaurants. Perhaps an ideal situation would be to stay in a Holiday Inn that had room service but was across the street from a Howard Johnson's that would be good for a late night snack!

Parking: This is a major consideration if you have rental cars, an equipment truck, or a load of instruments and equipment. Predictably, downtown hotels have limited parking, poor security, and frequently cannot accommodate oversize vehicles such as vans, trucks, or trailers, so you may want to stay farther out of town for higher security and convenience.

TIP

When parking in large city garages, it can sometimes take from 30 to 60 minutes to get your car during busy hours (New York City is famous for this). So if you're heading somewhere important, such as the concert, don't try to pick up the car from the garage at the last moment.

Checking of Equipment: If you have large quantities of equipment, which you must take with you, you'll need either a hotel with a secure checkroom (an older hotel service rapidly disappearing) or a motel where you can park near the door to your room for easy unloading. Don't take the location of the room for granted or you may find yourself lugging equipment up and down stairs and through long corridors or you may be forced to leave your belongings at great risk in the parking lot—an act not conducive to a good night's sleep.

=== TIP ===

Don't take chances with your equipment by leaving it in parked cars or vans. The hassles of a theft can be monumental, causing you to miss engagements as well as having to replace stolen items. Be sure to keep a list of the instrument serial numbers and descriptions so you can at least make a proper report of the stolen items, should it ever happen. In most large cities, stolen instruments get returned through pawn shops and music stores and can be recovered there if the police are given the serial numbers and descriptions.

Degree of Formality: The fanciest hotel in town may be ideal for the cultured voyager but may be less than comfortable for the professional on tour. Swanky hotels often require suit and tie in the dining room and may frown on show business types and their habits (having guests at all hours, practicing in the room, wearing colorful clothing, taking your latest lover to your room, etc.).

Attitude of Hotels: The attitude of hotel staff toward "show folk" can be very unpredictable. Most chain motels and large hotels don't seem to care about much except being paid, while locally run "mom and pop" places tend to take a more personal view of their tenants' habits and appearances. There's a comfortable, impersonal attitude at chain establishments that is perhaps preferable to too much interest in your comings and goings.

TIP

If you get a heavy snorer in the next room, try calling his room and then hang up when he answers. It's cruel, perhaps, but will probably give you time to get to sleep before he starts sawing logs again. If you get next to a pair of athletic lovers, then all you can do is try to enjoy the entertainment.

Creature Comforts: Although most hotels these days have such things as telephones and air conditioning, it is quite possible to wake up in a place without these and other commonly provided amenities, particularly in locally owned establishments. If you are traveling in a warm climate or in the habit of conducting a lot of business while you travel, take these possible inconveniences into consideration. This also applies to swimming pools and recreational facilities more important to some but welcomed by all if the stay is more than a few days.

Degree of Quiet: Some hotels have super-thin walls, making you an uninvited guest in your neighbor's activities.

TIP

A trick I learned from George Shearing is to carry around a small portable radio to drown out outside noises; I added my own twist, an earplug–great for those times when you find yourself in a hotel which has made no attempt at soundproofing and it seems like you're right on the test track.

TYPES OF LODGINGS
Hotels and motels can be arbitrarily divided into four general categories with some overlapping regarding cost. But be aware that

hotel rates are rising especially fast, many having doubled in the last five years. As with airlines, hotels are large energy users and are being priced upward faster than the general pace of inflation.

High Priced: Rooms in these hotels range from $60 and up per day ($90 and up in major cities such as Boston, L.A., New York, San Francisco, and Washington). The rooms and furnishings are nicer, the walls are more soundproof, and thorough, efficient service is offered. You can expect high prices on everything from tipping the bellhop to newspapers in the newsstand. Unfortunately, some of these establishments are complete rip-offs, offering a lot of pomp with lackluster service and overpriced everything, and they succeed in making the guest feel he is being done a favor by allowing him to stay in their hotel. Well-known hotels, like the St. Francis Hotel in San Francisco, The Ritz in Boston, and The Plaza in Copenhagen, to name a few, are the exceptions with their fine, well-deserved reputations.

Middle Priced: In this category of $35 to $50 per day ($50 to $75 in the large cities), one gets all the comforts and conveniences plus most of the advantages of higher priced hotels. Often there are no bellhops visible, but help is available if you need it, and prices all around are more reasonable. Instead of ordering that soft drink from room service where the tariff would be $1.50 plus tip, there is often a machine down the hall which will dispense the same for small change. Informal restaurants are also the expected fare. Unfortunately, discounts from the chain hotels and motels that predominate in this price range are hard to come by.

=========**TIP**=========

Of motels in this category my personal favorites are the Red Roof Inns.

Low Priced: The choice is between older hotels and lower quality motels in this category of the $25 to $35 room ($25 to $50 in larger cities). Although there are some very acceptable places at these rates, finding them is not always easy. Advertising is limited, so advice from someone local is suggested. Certain corners are cut, of course, to bring you a lower price: the room and furnishings may be a bit seedy; towels in short supply; heat may not be individually adjustable; air conditioning may not exist; telephone service, daytime only, if at all; black and white television, if any; no convenient restaurants; etc. But performer discounts are frequently available.

There are several new chains of low-priced motels springing up around the country (Susse Chalet, Day's Inn, Regal 8, Motel 6, Scot's Inn, etc.) If you're on a budget and don't mind staying outside of town where the properties aren't in prime neighborhoods, then get some of their brochures.

Long Term and Apartments: For extended stays of more than a week, you might be interested in an apartment hotel which offers an apartment with kitchen and is equipped with all the necessary housekeeping accoutrements, sometimes with daily maid service. Prices are comparable to a medium-priced hotel room but offer a lot more in spaciousness and facilities. These kinds of accommodations don't advertise much either, but are commonly found in both medium-sized and large cities. Discounts for professionals are rare.

If you'll be staying in one place for several weeks or months, then by all means search out someplace offering long-term lower rates at so much per week or month. This can be lower by as much as 30 to 50 percent of the daily rate normally charged.

RESERVATIONS
You should make reservations as much in advance as possible, especially in large cities or during holidays and the summer season. The local promoter can make the reservations for you or you can call direct or use the toll-free reservation number of the major chains. A guaranteed reservation is much better than the unconfirmed, which can be forefeited after 4 P.M. or just plain ignored by the hotel. To confirm a reservation, either send an advance deposit by check or give your credit card number. (See Appendix B for sample confirmation letter.) It is very reassuring to the weary traveler to know that there will be no hang-ups between you and your bed; accordingly, if you expect to arrive in the wee hours, when even a confirmed reservation can be uncertain, it is wise to telephone ahead.

Many hotels have a time such as midnight when even a guaranteed reservation will be given up if you haven't called to verify your late arrival. I found this out the hard way at about 1 A.M. one morning at a Sheraton Hotel near LaGuardia Airport.

Two of the companies which won't crassly give away your room if you're arriving late are Howard Johnson's and Holiday Inn. They will even get you a room at another hotel and provide transportation to it if they can't honor your guaranteed reservation.

TIP

To forestall a possible loss of room if you're arriving late, call the day of your reservation and ask the desk to mark your reservation card with your expected time of arrival. When cancelling a reservation, ask for a cancellation number for verification in case there's a dispute about it later.

As for *you* canceling on *them*, even a guaranteed reservation can be retracted without cost to you if cancelled before 4 o'clock on the same day you are to arrive. The one exception is hotels in resort areas which may charge a cancellation fee or one-day rental.

SPECIAL RATES
Staying in even a regular hotel for more than a week often qualifies you for special rates, which will save you as much as 10 to 20 percent of the daily rate. Discounts for show business people—the so-called professional rate—are frequently available from higher priced hotels (a substantial savings) and independently operated hotels (a few, but possibly important, dollars). For instance, the popular Bellvue Hotel in Hamburg is one such place offering a 10 percent discount to actors, TV and radio personalities, musicians, etc. Another hotel popular with performers is the Loew's La Cité Hotel in Montreal. It's a modern, highrise, excellent hotel with substantial discounts for performers if booked through the local promoter of your engagement in Montreal.

Sometimes simply asking in a positive manner while you are making the reservation will reap you a discount; other times only a local promoter with whom they are acquainted can make this work.

If you are part of a large group, you might qualify for a discount on the basis of quantity—the definition of which varies from one hotel to another. National chains are less likely to give special rates, but if you are booking a long tour of many cities, even they might consider it if you stay exclusively at their establishments on the tour.

CHECKING IN AND OUT

It might be a wise move to have the most respectable looking member of your group handle the check-in while the others wait in the car so that the hotel doesn't see what it's getting right away. It also speeds things along if only one person deals with the desk. Some hotels try to insist on individual registration, but this is not necessary unless each person is paying individually. Invariably the person registering will be asked for some sort of credit identification right away (credit cards other than gas or department store) or asked to pay in advance. With large groups you can send a list of names in advance and the hotel can preregister the members for a faster check-in.

TIP

It can speed things up to have Xeroxed lists of your personnel to use at each hotel so that the desk clerk, the hotel telephone operator, and each member of the group can have the room numbers. Just prepare a supply of name lists to take with you and fill in the room numbers when checking in.

If this is a downtown hotel or one with pretensions to grandeur, you'll be obligated to hire a bellhop to show you to your room even if you're only carrying the clothes on your back. He'll briskly whip into the room, turn on a few lights, and mumble something about the services of the hotel, for which you'll have to tip according to the distance to the room, the amount of baggage (50¢ to $1 per bag), and degree of posh.

SERVICES OFFERED

Some or all of the following services may be offered: (1) Messages held and forwarded. (2) Wake-up calls (though approximately one out of ten don't seem to materialize). (3) Telephone service with a local call surcharge ranging from 15¢ to 50¢ per call (some hotels have started a flat rate system, charging for unlimited local phone service whether you use it or not—hardly a fair arrangement to me). I recently stayed at the Hilton Hotel in Seattle where they added a surcharge on long distance calls as many foreign hotels do. It's a total rip-off for the hotel to do this and I hope it doesn't become common in the U.S. It's being phased out or reduced in Europe now so maybe it won't catch on here. (4) Laundry and dry cleaning (not on weekends or holidays, of course). (5) Checkroom for storage. (6) Room service. These waiters should get a tip of approximately 15 percent as with restaurant waiters. I usually tip a minimum of 75¢ to $1, with larger checks at 15 percent. Some hotels now automatically add the 15 percent tip to the bill, saving you the trouble. (7) A doorman who will watch or fetch your car or get you a taxi.

CHECKING OUT

Large city big hotels can be really a mess at morning check-out times with long lines and delays. In most cases, you can pay the bills the night before to avoid this. Expect to pay by cash or credit card, keeping in mind that large amounts will have to be okayed with your credit card company. New York City is the world's worst for having crowded check-out scenes. So allow extra time.

FOREIGN HOTELS

In the most Westernized of foreign countries you can expect accommodations similar to those in the U.S. But rooms in Europe and Japan tend to be small with less luxury, although this varies. Generally you will find that fewer towels, dimmer lighting, smaller beds, not-so-hot water, and such amenities as soap, face cloths, and tissue are limited.

Reservations can be made through a travel agent, your local contact, or directly by mail, Telex, or cable. In Europe and Japan, a reservation is a firm commitment, and if you fail to show, you are expected to pay for the first night.

Most establishments add a 10 to 15 percent service surcharge to all charges, although this extra tax doesn't go to the service people themselves and you may be expected to tip as well. The extra amount tipped is less than what is expected in the U.S.—5 to 10 percent—and sometimes nothing at all in smaller hotels. In Japan there is no tipping unless unusual service is provided.

There may be no free lunch these days, but there *is* free breakfast at many European and Japanese hotels. At the minimum, it is coffee and a roll—the so-called continental breakfast—at the maximum, something fit for a king. If breakfast is included in the room charge, it becomes more of a bargain and, I must say, a very civilized way to start the day.

Foreign countries are not used to the 24-hour-a-day life of Americans, so hours of opening and closing must be considered. Restaurants are often only open at mealtimes and reception desks not staffed at late hours. Keep informed for your own benefit. Wake-up calls are frequently, it would seem, put at the bottom of their priority lists. Consequently, don't trust this method of rising or you will find yourself missing early morning departures.

TIP

Virtually every experienced traveler I know carries an alarm clock. Hotel wake-up calls are just not reliable, especially in foreign hotels, it seems.

Also beware of making phone calls and having laundry and dry cleaning done, for virtually all foreign hotels add extremely high surcharges for these services. (I once had a dozen shirts and some underwear laundered in Hamburg, and the bill was $110—and that was in 1968! Last year in Switzerland, it happened again: $90 for some laundry.) A long distance call from Europe that costs $25 from a post office might cost $60 from a hotel. To avoid this, ask the party in the U.S. whom you're calling to call you back, thus making you subject to only a one-minute surcharge. The other alternative is to seek out the local post office and use one of the government phones. Even this costs more than if the call had been placed to you from the U.S., since U.S. rates are about the lowest in the world.

Most hotels overseas will exchange U.S. money for the local currency, and for small amounts this is practical, but their rate of exchange is very poor. Find an exchange bank or money changing house for converting larger amounts. Airport banks will exchange money too, but they don't offer quite as good rates as central offices downtown. Furthermore, when you return with foreign money, the exchange banks at U.S. airports give extremely poor rates. You're better off changing back into dollars before returning to the U.S., keeping in mind that some countries restrict how much you can change back (Italy and the Eastern European countries, for instance). (See Money section in Chapter 5 for more details.)

CHAPTER 4

HOW TO COPE WITH THE GIG

ADVANCE PLANNING

The best motto for touring is to "expect the unexpected." Since even missing one or two engagements on a tour can blow the profits and seriously hurt your reputation among promoters, it is important to plan carefully and anticipate problems. It is often possible to cope with last-minute crises and still make the gigs, but it's no fun to hang around airports for hours, to not have hotel rooms reserved, etc. Having everything run smoothly guarantees every likelihood of there being ample time to eat, rest, sound-check, and generally take care of business. And these things become incredibly important on a grueling tour. It's difficult to perform if you're in an ill-tempered, panicky state of mind because of travel hassles. Here are some general ideas and particulars on how to plan in advance.

AGENTS, MANAGERS, AND PROMOTERS

You'll be relying on agents, managers, and promoters for information, advance arrangements, and so on, not to mention getting paid.

Primarily, an agent's job is to make contact with buyers and arrange the booking of the performance. They negotiate the contract and take care of the paperwork related to the contract. Some also provide managerial-type services such as making travel arrangements and setting up publicity appearances, interviews, etc.

Usually, though, these more personalized services are done by a manager who will devote attention to personal travel plans, performance details (staging requirements, for instance), promotion of your career, and often handle your finances as well. Some people in the business act as combined agent-managers, providing all the required services.

There is also a choice between having an exclusive agreement with an agency or manager or working with several different agencies for different types of bookings or in different geographical locations. The right choice depends upon the individual career.

The promoter, of course, is the person who sponsors the performance. Sometimes it might be a large organization or institution, such as a university, or it could be a one-man operation in a smaller location or a commercial establishment such as a club or restaurant. In any event you'll ultimately be dependent on the promoter for providing much of what you'll require for a successful performance, not the least of which is an audience attracted by advertising and publicity.

So, by all means, develop an understanding of how various promoters handle their responsibilities so you'll know what to expect when you arrive in a town for an engagement. And stay in touch. The more you explain what you want, the more likely the promoter will come through for you.

THE CONTRACT

Most groups will use some form of the union contract for negotiating their services. (See Appendix D for sample.) Without a signed agreement you have no legal or union-backed recourse should you not get paid. The contract has several copies, one of which is supposed to be sent to the musicians' union that has local jurisdiction over the location you are playing. This is called "filing" the contract. The union locals vary on their attitude about this: most aren't too strict, while a few are very fussy. The union needs a copy of the contract and will charge you a few dollars for work dues.

TIP

Always have a copy of the contract with you at the job in case the union representative appears and wants one.

The contract will spell out the necessary facts of the job: (1) the name of the group, (2) the promoter, his address, and phone numbers, (3) time and place of performance, (4) length of time to be performed, (5) amount of payment in advance deposit, if any, (6) amount to be paid at performance, (7) form of payment (specified as cash, certified check, cashier's check, or university check), (8) amount percentage, if any.

A typical contract, for example, might list a $1,000 deposit sent in advance, a $1,000 payment at time of performance plus 60 percent of the gross over $5,000. If the gross is $8,000, that leaves a balance of $3,000 in excess of $5,000, and 60 percent of $3,000 is $1,800. So a total of $2,800 is to be collected at the performance, over and above the $1,000 sent in advance. Most contracts, even those which do not include a percentage deal, will show the potential maximum gross income of the performance on the contract.

If a percentage is involved, the promoter will provide you with a box office statement to verify the figures. Depending on the circumstances, there are a variety of ways for the promoter to manipulate the evidence, from not reporting the ticket numbers properly to changing the seating in the hall to a larger number than stated on the contract. My advice is to check as carefully as you can, depending on the cooperation of the promoter, and consider what you determine to be the likelihood of being treated fairly. (Groups that perform regularly for large audiences generally assign someone, like a road manager, to check tickets, keep records, and so on to be certain of an accurate count.) *Note*: If working primarily "for the door," or a percentage, watch out for free guests of the club owner/promoter.

DEPOSITS

It is sometimes a slow process to get a promoter to send a deposit. Of course you could cancel, but if your tour is set up and you don't want to lose the date, you have to decide how far to trust the promoter. If he is well-established, then he might just be casual about sending deposits. If you're uncertain, try to get at least a small deposit—it shows the good faith of the promoter.

RIDERS

Besides the regular contract, both the performer and/or the promoter may have additional requirements in the form of a rider attached to the contract. (See Appendix D for sample rider.) Some things possibly included in artist riders: (1) equipment the promoter will provide (risers, sound, lights, instruments, etc.), (2) piano tuner or rental, (3) restrictions on broadcasting or tape recording the performance, (4) providing local ground transportation, (5) billing status and advertising of the performance, and (6) refreshments to be provided.

The promoter's rider ordinarily includes such things as: (1) restrictions against performing in their area (usually a distance of 50 to 100 miles surrounding the city of the concert during a period of 30 to 60 days prior to their concert), (2) limitations on their liabilities in case the concert has to be canceled because of strikes, weather, etc., (3) assigning employer status to the band leader so the responsibility for any employer taxes is placed on the band leader and not on the promoter, and (4) restrictions on the behavior of the musicians regarding such things as foul language, use of narcotics, and even alcoholic beverages on some college campuses (even against smoking on campus at Brigham Young University in Mormon country).

TIP

Many details of riders are loosely followed or completely ignored by promoters. This is a condition caused by ridiculously complicated riders running 30 or 40 pages listing irrelevant things. Conditions vary from one engagement to another so not all items might be appropriate. My suggestion is to list separately in a letter the most important items you require and even follow up with a telephone call to check on these things. Many promoters barely glance at lengthy riders unless they've heard the performer is particularly difficult to deal with.

POSSIBLE TANGLES

You may find yourself working exclusively through a certain booking agent or manager/agent. Or you may work with several different agents from time to time. Sometimes agents work in cooperation with other agents as well so it often gets confusing as to who is responsible for various details. Some agents are infamous for letting details go unattended, leaving the performer and the promoter to slug it out over the details the night of the performance. If you're dealing with an agent you don't know, there could even be problems getting the deposit money after the concert. Some are pretty loose.

If you find that your agent needs a manager himself, then for your own protection, stay in touch with the local promoter. Don't be afraid to contact the local promoter yourself after the job is booked if you aren't getting the answers to your questions about the details of the performance. This is especially necessary if you are relying on the promoter to provide instruments, equipment, or transportation.

LAST-MINUTE BARGAINING

Although everyone would like to have big crowds at every job, on occasion, eleventh-hour negotiations may go on if a promoter is experiencing very low ticket sales. It's up to you whether you want to work for a lower fee or cancel completely. It may depend on how big a hole the cancellation will leave in your tour schedule and whether there is enough bargaining room in your fee to allow for adjustment. If it's a promoter you hope to work with again or feel sympathetic towards, then adjustment is usually wise. However, if you feel the promoter hasn't done his job of advertising or is so big that he should be able to afford the loss easily, then insist on the full amount. You still might find the concert canceled, even with a contract. But you may, at least, get to keep the deposit money. More about gigs that get cancelled or go unpaid later.

GETTING PAID AFTER THE GIG

Promoters sometimes don't adhere to the payment procedure stipulated in the contract. Even though the contract may state cash, it's possible you will be offered any one of a number of substitutes instead, so if you need cash, suggest how much and specify in what form you want to receive the balance. Accept *anything but* personal checks.

Only a few promoters can be trusted to the extent of issuing personal checks for payments. If you can't do anything about it, use your judgment based on the promoter's reputation in the business, etc. Good ones won't offer one to you, so be cautious if it's suggested. I have had problems with personal checks three times in my career and every time I could sense something was fishy—use your instincts.

Incidentally, if you have trouble getting paid at the job or soon thereafter, you may not get paid in the end. If nothing happens after a short wait, and assuming you have a contract, contact the union local having jurisdiction in the area. (If you failed to mail the union representatives a copy of the contract in advance, claim you sent it to the wrong address or something to keep their assistance.) They may have some sway over promoters in their area, but if there's any dispute between you and a promoter don't always expect help, because they might be more friendly with a promoter or club owner they've known for years than with a stranger from out of town. If you've been paid by check and it bounces, that is illegal, so you have some advantage. Now, the bad news: unless the amount in question is several thousand or more, it won't pay to take legal action. Even if you win, the legal fees will probably exceed the settlement, and if the guy doesn't have any money, you still won't get anything. He'll just disappear or declare bankruptcy, for instance.

So in spite of all the authority of contracts, unions, etc., a gig contract is only as good as the parties signing it. Know who you're dealing with, and if the party you're relying on seems untrustworthy, then be ready for anything.

CHECKLISTS

Because of the many complications that a group of touring musicians can run into, I have found that devising a series of checklists is very helpful in planning a tour, and in avoiding any possible snags during it. By utilizing such a series of lists, you are prepared in advance for most hassles, your tour will run more smoothly, and you will come out ahead. See Appendix A for the checklists I use, and on which you can base yours.

EQUIPMENT ON TOUR

Concepts of the quality of equipment and the delicateness of instruments vary widely among people. Most nonmusicians can't fully appreciate the consequences of poor equipment or easily damaged instruments. So when a promoter is providing borrowed or rented equipment there is always a risk.

In many years of observing other people's equipment I've seen some amazing things, such as a bass fiddle we once were provided in Bordeaux, France. It was homemade from plywood, about half-size, not yet finished (as if it were taken off the workbench for the performance), and it had only three strings! Needless to say, we had to do some fast looking for a real instrument to play.

Another bass story that demonstrates the layperson's lack of appreciation for instruments took place in a hotel lobby many years ago. Our bassist had his instrument out of the case, waiting to go into a ballroom to perform. As we were standing there, we noticed an aged gentleman shuffling across the hotel lobby on his way to the elevator. As he passed the bass, he stopped and looked at it for a second and then removed his wad of chewing gum and stuck it on the bass! Then he turned to us standing there dumbfounded and said, "Hey, I stuck muh gum on your machine there!" We could barely react at first and then finally couldn't stop laughing.

So be careful how you leave your instruments lying around, particularly between the soundcheck and the performance. Try to have someone stay at the hall with equipment until performance time.

Unfortunately, my instrument, the vibraphone, lends itself to abuse. Stagehands are tempted to play on it with screwdrivers and other tools, and people use it as a table for their drinks, etc. Once I came into a club I was working and found an opening act singer doing a Sophie Tucker number actually sitting on the vibes as she sang her song! Too bad it managed to hold her weight.

While I'm on the subject, I'll mention one of my pet gripes. That is when people go up to concert grand pianos and pound out their favorite songs or simply thump on the piano's low notes to hear the sound of the bass strings. Ask any pianist and he'll tell you that improper playing of a fine piano can easily affect the action and tuning and is not recommended. For some unfortunate reason, musicians who have great sensitivity about their own instruments feel perfectly free to abuse pianos as if they're community property and indestructible. They should show some consideration for the pianists who will have to perform on the instrument after they've been at it.

RENTAL POSSIBILITIES

Sometimes equipment will have to be rented from local music stores or instrument rental companies located in larger cities. The cost of such rentals can be substantial, but it is often preferable to carrying things like electric pianos or heavy amplifiers on complicated or extended tours. If the promoter is renting the equipment for you, make sure it is clear who is paying for it *and* be certain of the brand and quality. In some cases the promoter may be tempted to cut corners and end up providing unreliable equipment.

=== TIP ===

When rental equipment is being provided, try to do the soundcheck as early in the day as possible so as to allow time for getting other instruments in case the first ones don't work right.

REPAIRS

Getting equipment repaired is fairly easy in large cities and nearly impossible in small ones. A good procedure is to call the local music stores to see if they can assist you. Also ask local musicians for advice on where to go. If nothing is working, call the home office of the instrument manufacturer and tell them your problem. They will at least know their dealers in your area and might even contact them for you to request that they offer all possible assistance. Most musical instrument companies are sympathic to musicians on the road who use their instruments because there is no better advertisement possible for their product.

TIP

Get in the habit of carrying along spare parts and tools for the instruments you use. Things like fuses, ground plug adapters, spare cords, mending tape and wire, solder and soldering gun for electronic equipment, replacement parts for piano notes, tuning hammer for acoustic piano, spare drum heads, light oil, etc.

FOREIGN ELECTRICITY

This is another problem that you should deal with before you go abroad. Europe, Great Britain, and Japan all have different currents, and their outlets and plugs are not interchangeable either. Virtually *no* European hall or studio has adapters or transformers and you'll need both for American-made equipment. As for plugs, the Belgians, French, and Spanish use one kind; Austrians, and Germans another; Swiss, another; and the British and Japanese, yet two other kinds. A complete set of adapter plugs can often be purchased from airport travel notions counters or from large city hardware stores. The most common brand I've seen is made by the Franzus Company.

Besides the plug adapters, you will also need a transformer to match the current in the country you expect to visit. (Europe is 220, 60 cycles; Japan is 110, 50 cycles.) These can be purchased in the U.S. in electrical supply houses but are not commonly found in hardware stores. In Europe transformers can be found in some hardware stores and some department stores such as the Printemps in Paris, but they are far more expensive than those bought in the U.S. You can expect to pay $50 or more for a suitable transformer.

Beware of the small power converter which some companies like

Franzus offer for small appliances. These are adequate for hair dryers and electric razors, but transistorized equipment like amplifiers will only sizzle.

In addition, if you have a *lot* of electronics, don't use just one transformer or you may overload. Also fuses seem to blow easier in Europe than in the States. So to avoid a large strain on the fusebox, have your electrical equipment switched on before you plug the transformer into the hall's outlet.

FOREIGN TOURS

A passport for each person is an absolute necessity and can be acquired on as little as one week's notice from a passport agency in most major cities. But if you have the time, allow a month to six weeks. The requirements are that you present an original birth certificate (photocopies are not acceptable), two passport photographs, which can usually be obtained after a brief wait from passport photo shops in the vicinity of the passport office, and a small cash fee. Passports come in various sizes, that is, number of pages. If you expect considerable travel, then request a greater number of pages.

Guard your passport and all visa papers carefully. The officials do not replace lost ones easily, and if you lose one in the middle of a tour, you'll probably have to go home instead of finishing the tour. My only near miss with a passport happened a few years ago in Austria. I left my passport in my hotel in Munich, taking the train to Austria for a concert. I had mixed up another musician's passport with mine and thought my own was securely in my pocket. At the border, I absent-mindedly handed it to the inspector; he glanced at it and handed it back not noticing it wasn't my picture. On the return trip back to Germany, I noticed it wasn't mine. So did the inspector this time! I tried to explain it and make it believable. His very words were, "Well, I can choose to believe you or I can choose not to believe you." Finally, he chose to believe me (whew!) and let me back into Germany. Needless to say, I'm ultra-careful with my passport these days.

Visas and working papers are prerequisites for entry into some countries. At the moment Canada, Great Britain, Switzerland, Yugoslavia, and Japan are among those that require them. The local promoter will usually advise you if either is required, but to be on the safe side, make sure to ask. They may be obtained from the consulate of the country in question *before* the tour begins. Once the promoter from the country involved has sent in the proper papers, some visas can be obtained after a wait of one or two days. Usually you will be notified that a visa is ready for you to pick up. However, in many cases it can take up to a month or more, so try to allow plenty of lead time. *In most cases you cannot obtain either working permits or visas once you have arrived in the country.*

A carnet registering equipment and instruments will probably be necessary in order to cross borders, especially in Europe where many bands have literally been turned away at the border when trying to enter the strictest of countries: France, some Scandinavian countries, Yugoslavia, and Eastern European countries. (See Carnet Applications in Chapter 5.)

Hotel and hall locations are difficult to find in many cities overseas, especially if this is your first tour there. If you are driving, you can get frustratingly wound up in the traffic and narrow streets.

TIP

If you have difficulty with the maps you have, then try the taxi trick: have one of your cohorts get in a taxi and proceed to the destination while you follow in your car. It also helps if the name of the place is written out in large, clear letters, for in case of a language lapse, even a slight mispronunciation can confuse and cause mistakes.

Check travel conditions carefully. Sometimes planes and trains have the oddest rules, and roads in foreign countries can be exceptionally tricky. For example, some years ago the equipment truck of a band I know decided to take a direct but small highway to another city, only to somehow get wedged in a mountain crevass that the road went through but no truck ever could. After turning back to start again on another route, the truck missed the concert.

Once again, in foreign countries reservations for flights need to be reconfirmed at each stopover lasting longer than 72 hours or your reservation may be canceled. This is also true if you make any changes in your flight plan. A few airports still charge what they call an airport tax, which is a few dollars collected prior to boarding. Save some of the local currency for this tax. This could be a great spot to unload some of the otherwise useless coins or currency—the leftovers too small for banks to accept for conversion.

Be aware that many countries abroad have strict rules regarding how much cash you can carry across the border and restrictions on how much of their currency you can change back into dollars. (Italy, Yugoslavia, and Japan are forerunners in the latter situation.) Some simply have limitations on how much of *any* country's cash you can carry out. If you do have to carry a large sum through a border, convert your cash into cashier's checks at American bank branches (see Chapter 5), but if this is impossible, by all means be inconspicuous.

Foreign countries' business offices have sometimes unpredictable hours. Nothing much is open on Saturday afternoons or Sundays in Europe. A few (like in Portugal, Spain, Yugoslavia) may have a long lunch-hour closing and then stay open until seven or eight in the evening. Moral: Don't wait until the last minute to do business, make plane ticket changes, go to the post office, and so on.

CANADIAN TOURS

Canadian customs and immigration now require some advance preparation. You should allow up to one hour for crossing the border, and you are sometimes obligated to acquire a work permit in advance of the job through your Canadian promoter or consulate.

The equipment and instruments you will take should be itemized on a list giving serial numbers, brand names, and approximate value for the purpose of bonding. A bond, arranged through the promoter, from a customs bonding agent *or* cash deposit must be left at the border to insure that your equipment won't be sold in Canada. Have about a half-dozen Xerox copies of your equipment list (see Appendix B.)

The cash security deposit is arbitrarily determined by the customs official you will be dealing with, but it is usually in the vicinity of 25 percent of the value you declare on your instruments and equipment. My suggestion is to declare a fairly low value, particularly if you have used instruments, so that your security deposit is not prohibitively high. Once you have returned to the United States and it is verified that you have all your equipment, your deposit will be mailed to you. Unfortunately, even if you pay in U.S. dollars, your refund will be mailed in Canadian dollars, thereby costing you an approximate 15 percent devaluation in currency exchange. Plus, to add insult to injury, when you deposit the Canadian check in your account, the bank will charge you an additional fee for clearing a foreign check.

The Canadian customs officer may or may not decide to hit you up for a bond or deposit. It's very unpredictable. I usually stop at American customs as I leave the U.S. and get a "temporary export permit" for the equipment I'm taking out of the U.S. The U.S. customs officer simply takes a copy of our equipment list and stamps it. Then when I go to Canadian customs they tend to look favorably on the fact that the U.S. officials have a registered list of the equipment and are more likely to forego the security deposit. When returning to the U.S., turn in the temporary export permit at customs, and they too will be unlikely to give you a detailed enquiry about your equipment.

If you take promotional materials, such as records or posters, expect that Canada will charge you duty. It might be easier not to bring them with you.

Also at the Canadian border, the immigration officer will check the group members' IDs and work permits, issuing temporary admission papers for all people. If there are more than four, a single paper will list them all. At this time tell them if any group member is planning to leave Canada separately; then an extra copy of this paper, called a "manifest," can be made up for each member traveling separately.

Some types of work in Canada require advance paperwork on the part of the Canadian promoter, in addition to visas and work permits. Be sure to check on this before you go, and allow time to get it through a Canadian consul. Visas require proof of identity, such as passport or birth certificate, ID photographs, and filled-out forms. Work permits in Canada are included with the visa after the Canadian promoter gets official permission to offer you employment.

Finally, 15 percent of the gross from your engagement is withheld by the Canadian tax people. Your employer sends it in and at year's end sends you a form showing it was withheld. You can claim it on your U.S. tax as a credit, so eventually you do get it back. You can get the withholding reduced or canceled by going to the local tax office in Canada and showing your expenses (salaries, travel costs, hotel bills, etc.)

By all means make certain you get something in writing from the promoter to verify that he is withholding tax. At the very least a letter from him giving the details.

=============**TIP**=============

I suggest getting at least a letter about the tax from the promoter at the time of the performance. At the end of the year, it might be hard to track the promoter down if he's gone out of business or moved.

CHAPTER 5

THINGS TO SIMPLIFY YOUR LIFE ON TOUR

MONEY TRANSACTIONS

CASH

Having sufficient cash to meet road expenses is an ongoing problem. Of course no one wants to carry large amounts of cash, but better to have too much than too little. Try to plan ahead what expenses you may need, meeting the possible cash needs of band members along the road, and schedule when you can pick up additional money during the tour. Do your best to keep some in reserve in case of the unexpected: a cash fee may turn out to be in the form of a check or fail to materialize at all, and bad weather occasionally cancels a performance.

Beware of trying to spend large denominations, even fiftys. Banks often won't change hundreds or fiftys unless you have an account with them, nor will hotels sometimes, unless they happen to have large amounts on hand.

It isn't easy to get cash sent to you on the road. Western Union money transfers are possible, but delays of several hours are also possible. The person sending must go in person to send it and the one receiving must go to the main office to claim the money. Large sums—anything over several hundred dollars—may be ruled out depending on the cash on hand at the telegraph-receiving office. They are not obligated to pay in cash, although they will usually have at least some cash on hand to offer as partial payment, with the rest in a Western Union money order which is usually fairly easy to cash, except perhaps at night or on Sundays or holidays.

A couple of years ago, I returned from a concert and opened the door to my hotel room, and found to my astonishment, an elderly gentleman sitting there in a bathrobe watching television. At first I thought I had somehow walked into the wrong room. However, I could see all my things lying there and knew I wasn't wrong. The man looked at me in amazement and said, "Where's Art?"

"Art who," I countered.

"Isn't this Art's room?," he asked getting a little concerned.

"No, I don't think so."

"Well, I guess I'd better go then and find Art," he said as he took his things and wandered off down the hall.

I suppose the desk gave him the wrong key to his friend's room, and he sat in my room for several hours waiting for Art. It does show you how lax security can be in hotel rooms and how easy it would be for someone to get into a room if they wanted.

Individual safe-deposit boxes found in some hotels should be reasonably safe.

I did walk up to a hotel counter in Japan last year and discover a safety deposit box key lying there. I gave it to the person in charge, but they misunderstood and thought that it was my own key. They brought me a deposit box, as I protested, that was full of money and papers, which must have belonged to whoever had inadvertently left his key. What with the language barrier, it took me about five minutes to convince them it wasn't mine. Be advised that some hotel safes can only be opened by the manager. I once waited with George Shearing's band several hours for the manager to arrive so we could get our hard-earned cash stored in the safe and get on with our trip.

CASHIER'S CHECKS

Cashier's checks or bank money orders can be purchased at any bank in the U.S. and at American branch banks abroad. The charge is minimal—from 25¢ to $1 (slightly more abroad)—and it is a very simple and quick procedure. You can be safe carrying it with you or sending it through the mail. The bank can stop payment and reissue if there are any slip-ups; just save the receipt until you cash it.

But don't let bank tellers deceive you about the "cashability" of a cashier's check. Virtually no bank will cash one unless you have an account with them. In addition, not all banks will cash it on the spot, even if you do have an account; banks in the East will give it several days to a week to clear; banks in the Middle and Far West will give an immediate clearance, as a rule.

=== TIP ===

When sending any check for deposit to your bank, endorse it, and add "for deposit only" plus the name of your bank.

CERTIFIED CHECKS

These are merely personal checks which the bank certifies as good by setting aside money for payment when due. It is as reliable as a cashier's check or cash; the only difference is the few days to a week to wait for clearance on a certified check.

TIP

American Express offers emergency traveler's checks up to $500 per week from machines placed in most major airports in the U.S. It is a very helpful service and one of the big attractions for having an American Express card. (See Credit Cards later in this chapter.)

TRAVELER'S CHECKS

These can be purchased at any bank or American Express office for a small surcharge. They are sometimes handy to have on the road and are another good way of sending money to your account while out of town. Just fill them in payable to yourself, and endorse "for deposit only" to your bank. Remember to keep the serial number list separate from the checks in case you need a loss refund, and remember that large denominations are just as hard to change as large bills.

FOREIGN MONEY

The first hassle of foreign travel is always having the correct local currency. To give you enough for small expenses, exchange some at the airport or the border. Most hotels will change money, but their rate is not nearly so good as a major bank. In banks, the larger the amount, the better the exchange rate. Note that small coins won't be accepted for exchange.

Do be careful: it is always easy to change *into* the local cash, but not always the other way around. Many countries will only do so if you can produce a receipt showing how you obtained the local currency; plus many have a maximum limit (say, $100) for exchange back into dollars. The countries with the freest exchange rules are Belgium, Germany, Luxemburg, Switzerland, and to a lesser extent, Scandinavia. Restricted countries are France, Italy, Spain, and Yugoslavia.

You can always take the money out of the country with you and

THINGS TO SIMPLIFY YOUR LIFE ON TOUR 97

exchange it at your next stop (except with Eastern European monies which are not accepted for exchange in Western countries). But be aware that many countries have laws prohibiting removal of *their* currency, except in small amounts; Italy is an example.

It is not uncommon to find yourself having to carry out fairly large amounts of currency from these countries if you have been playing engagements there, and performers do it all the time. But by all means be discreet about how you carry the money and take precautions against it being readily discovered during the security check before boarding the plane, for instance. Generally American travelers are not given much scrutiny, but it is a violation of their laws, and I don't really know how complicated it might become should one be apprehended with a large sum of money upon departure.

=== TIP ===

Don't expect to buy gasoline, meals, pay tolls, etc., unless you have the local currency. The easy acceptability of Canadian and U.S. dollars back and forth across the border in North America is not so common in Europe. Plan ahead to get the local currency, especially if you'll be changing countries late at night or on Sunday when the currency exchange offices at the border might be closed.

CASHIER'S AND OTHER CHECKS
The best countries for converting cash into cashier's and traveler's checks are Belgium, Germany, Holland, and Switzerland. There are American branch banks in most of their major cities which can handle this kind of transaction. First National City Bank, Chemical Bank, and American Express Banks are the most numerous. A local European bank might agree to issue you a check in exchange for your cash, but it may take them several days or longer; if you want it sent directly to your stateside bank, it can take a month or two for clearance.

At an American bank branch, a few minutes is all you'll need to get a cashier's check in dollars. They first convert your cash into the local currency, as required by law, and then convert it to U.S. dollars to issue the check. The charge is not substantial, but more than a similar U.S. transaction since you are paying for the currency conversion as well. Converting several thousand into a cashier's check can cost as much as $40 or $50. Still, it's worth it to be free from worrying when carrying around large amounts.

TIP

The quickest way to send money home from Europe is definitely through an American bank branch. Purchase a cashier's check and mail it express mail to your bank or home. Sending the money by wire is also very quick but more expensive. The first way might take a total of three to five days, and wiring could be a couple of days. Administrative delays will slow down the process when you transfer money through the bank's own channels or use a European bank with no American offices. It can take several weeks.

MAIL SERVICE

U.S. MAIL

There will be occasions when you will need to send money, checks, or important papers through the mail. Although sending cash is a bad idea, you can send it registered and be reasonably certain it will arrive.

Regular first class is relatively fast, although some letters mysteriously take a week or more. Special Delivery is not as great as it sounds. Until the letter reaches the city of destination, it travels as any other first class piece, and only when it gets there does it receive any special treatment. This special carrier delivery includes Sundays and holidays, and only thereby can be called an improvement.

The U.S. Postal Service also offers one-day "guaranteed" delivery from large city main offices. If you are in dire straits because you need a written message to be delivered the next day, take it in person before midafternoon to your main post office. The fee starts at $7 plus postage. I advise calling for details first, but they do guarantee its delivery with the next day's mail. (By guaranteeing delivery, they simply mean they will refund your fee if they blow it. Not much risk on their part, of course. They don't guarantee your losses if your business deal falls through because your contract, for instance, didn't arrive in time.)

AIR OR BUS DELIVERY SERVICE
Another way to send small items, packets, or letters is via air or bus lines. The cost is considerable for this small package service, but emergencies sometimes make it necessary. And it's extremely quick—I once got a passport which had been left behind in a few hours. Federal Air Express advertises a lot and has door-to-door service. Regular passenger airlines include small parcel service, but the package has to be taken and picked up at the airport in person.

FOREIGN MAIL
In some European countries and Japan this is very reliable and you can expect a letter to be received in a few days' time. I suggest Air Mail Express for speed and safety. Germany, Switzerland, Austria, Holland, and Scandinavia have the best postal systems in Europe, but I wouldn't trust Italy, Spain, Portugal, Belgium, or the Eastern European countries with an important letter. France and Great Britain are dependable but a little slower than should be.

You will find postal rates overseas much higher than what we are used to. For example, an Air Mail Express letter from Switzerland to the U.S. can cost as much as $1.50 versus 50¢ to 75¢ the other way.

CREDIT CARDS

Sometimes hard for musicians to acquire, these "passages to freedom" are both a blessing and a curse. Credit cards can encourage excess spending in the most conservative of people; however, they are a great boon in emergency situations and offer a sense of security when traveling and doing business of any kind. My suggestion is to restrict your use of them to only expenses that you have planned for in your budget or for emergencies. My approach is to pay road expenses in cash whenever possible so that credit card bills don't get out of hand.

To be eligible for any credit card, you must have some yearly income to report. If you live at home with your parents and/or earn less than a few thousand a year, then it is out of the question unless a family member or business associate will obtain one for you. (For this they would be legally responsible for your bills, but they would also be doing you a tremendous favor by helping you get started with a credit history.)

BANK CREDIT CARDS

The largest number of credit cards in circulation are the bank-issued credit cards such as Master Charge and Visa. Both are obtainable through banks and are easier to get than the prestige cards which specialize in travel and entertainment. If you maintain checking and saving accounts at a bank for a time and are known as a reliable account holder, you probably qualify for a bank credit card (assuming you have steady work).

When asked to state your profession or employment, it is best to avoid the word "musician" if possible. One substitute, if you are employed as a free-lance musician, is to say you work for a concert promoter doing publicity work or public relations or you organize concerts. If you have any other interests of a part-time nature, stress your other credentials. Say you're in the publishing business if you have published any songs or are a teacher if you give lessons. (See Credit Rating in Chapter 6.)

Once you are approved for a card, you will find there is a limit on the balance you can charge based on your financial state. This limit may be anywhere from $250 up to $1,500. You will have the option of paying your charges in full each month or making payment on the installment plan at very high interest rates. The latter is how the banks profit most from their cards. Most customers end up spreading out their account balance payments over several months, contributing a handsome profit to the bank. In addition the banks are paid a small percentage commission by the merchants from whom you made the purchase.

There is a yearly fee for having some bank credit cards ($10 to $20, for instance), and you can charge anything and everything from travel tickets to hotels and merchandise worldwide.

TRAVEL AND ENTERTAINMENT CREDIT CARDS

Cards such as American Express, Diner's Club, and Carte Blanche have four main differences between them and bank cards: (1) They are harder to acquire, and many applicants are turned down. A minimum of $12,500 to $15,000 yearly income is expected, and self-employed people probably have to show an even larger income or a secure financial situation, such as owning a house, etc. (2) There is a yearly membership fee of approximately $35 per person. (3) There is no set limit on the account balance you can charge, although large charges have to be okayed by phone with the company when you make a purchase. And depending on your history of payment and your general credit history, you might be turned down on an excessive amount. (4) All bills have to be paid in full each month.

Another advantage other than prestige—the importance of which varies from one person to the next—is that there are emergency cash possibilities, particularly with American Express. American Express has over 1,000 offices worldwide, giving you more on-the-spot service in case of lost cards and cash needs. In emergencies, they offer up to $800 in traveler's checks and, depending on the currency regulations of some countries, up to $200 in cash.

A big plus: American Express has placed machines in most major U.S. airports, dispensing to their card holders up to $500 per week in traveler's checks 24 hours a day. This extra service is available by requesting a code number and instructions from the company. If you use the machine procedure, the amount will automatically be noted as drawn from your checking account so be sure to maintain the necessary balance.

The travel and entertainment credit card companies are competing heavily in offering new services. American Express and Diner's Club are the most innovative. Diner's has a two-card, double account system so you can easily separate business from personal expenses, and they offer $75,000 automatic flight insurance on airline tickets charged on their card.

American Express also offers $75,000 flight insurance on tickets purchased with the card and provides the most opportunities for emergency money while away from home with their many offices and cash machines.

New services and advantages are being concocted all the time, so you'll frequently hear about new additions.

AUTO RENTAL CARDS
Car rental companies offer credit cards too, and while such rentals can be charged on bank or travel and entertainment cards, there are two distinct advantages to having their cards. With the major companies you are assigned a number identifying your license information, address, insurance preferences, and type of car you prefer, so the rental contract and car are ready and waiting when you are. And

you will be billed directly by the rental company, thereby not adding that charge to the balance on your other card (helpful if there's a limit on your credit credit card).

Occasionally it's possible to get a business discount (up to 20 percent) from the major rental companies. If you are associated, even remotely, with any large concern (if you teach at a university, record for a record company, or work part-time with a major firm), then you can probably get a credit card which automatically takes 20 percent off your charges (except for specials or discount rentals).

Remember that APA and AAA offer their members 30 percent discounts on car rentals.

=== TIP ===

Avis will accept Hertz credit cards for rentals, but Hertz will not accept Avis credit cards. They all accept American Express, Diner's Club, Visa, Master Charge, etc.

TELEPHONE CREDIT CARDS

These are only available if you have a solid relationship with the phone company. These cards allow you to make long distance calls from pay phones, hotels, or any phone to be charged to your home phone account. This speeds things up and avoids collect calls and calls to your home for verification. For someone who does a lot of phone work, it is a great convenience. You can also use them in a number of European countries for calls to the States.

PROBLEMS WITH ERRORS OR LOST CARDS

The new laws regarding credit card protection are a considerable guarantee against your being taken advantage of by errors or unauthorized use. In the case of errors in billing, notify the company in writing within 60 days and withhold payment of the disputed charge. They will correct the error or explain it to your satisfaction, and they cannot threaten your credit while the dispute is being settled.

As great as credit cards are when they work, billing errors can be a real problem, although with perseverance things can usually be straightened out. I've been trying to get a billing error with American Express cleared up for six months, with a multitude of misunderstanding on the part of various company employees *and* the computer, but I have great expectations.

Even stranger was an incident I had with Diner's. I stopped my Diner's Club account in 1967, but in 1973 or 1974 I got a bill for 89¢! I called to explain that I didn't have an account with them, etc., etc., and would they please take care of it. Their move was to send me a new account and credit card (which I returned). I wouldn't be too surprised to be billed the 89¢ again some day.

In case a card is lost or stolen, immediately notify the company. Telephone them and also send written notification, such as a telegram. The law states that once written notice is received, your liability closes. Once they've received your notice, you are not responsible for any unauthorized charges. Even for unauthorized charges *before* they get the notice, you are liable for only the first $50.

TIP

As a final reminder, keep a list of all your credit cards and numbers separate from your wallet for easy reporting in case of loss. (See Appendix B for Personal Information form to be kept on your person at all times.)

COMMUNICATIONS

TELEPHONE

Service and quality vary widely from country to country. It is generally assumed that the U.S. and Canada have the best service in the world—it certainly is the cheapest. In Europe, Germany and Switzerland have the highest quality services, and most of the others, with the exception of France, Italy, Portugal, Spain, and Yugoslavia, are reliable if nothing else.

Direct dial equipment, interconnecting not only most of Europe and Great Britain but the U.S. and Canada as well, has been installed in all but certain smaller towns. In these places where an operator must be used, a call can take as much as an hour or two to complete during business hours, instead of the usual few seconds.

Undoubtedly, the most notoriously frustrating phone service in Europe is in France and Italy, where constant interference with connections, wrong numbers, dead phones, and high prices abound.

Coin telephones in foreign countries can also be baffling. It seems as if each country has dreamed up its own mystery machine for this purpose. Great Britain's are among the most confusing because you cannot put the money in until your party answers and yet you cannot hear any words. When a faint beeping noise comes on the line, you quickly deposit your money, presuming that someone has answered and is patiently waiting. In Germany and Switzerland, you deposit coins in advance and as your call progresses your money is credited; however, any excess is not refunded. The German pay phones, especially the newer models, definitely win the prize for being the most impressive machines in this category.

Within Europe, telephone calls are not unusually expensive. Charges are based on how many minutes you talk with no minimum time requirements, such as the three-minute minimum used by the American telephone company. However, a transatlantic call is considerably more if placed in Europe rather than in the U.S. If you are initiating the call, make it collect or have the party you are calling in the U.S. hang up and call you back. *Beware of large surcharges levied on calls made from hotels, as this can more than double the cost of your call. Place it instead from a post office or private residence or call collect.*

Microwave telephone service is one of the latest developments in telephone communications. One non-Bell Telephone long distance system in the field is Southern Pacific Communications. They operate their independent microwave lines in a majority of the major cities in the U.S. If you call major cities a great deal, this might be of interest to you since the cost of their long distance calls is considerably cheaper than that of Bell's, it costs nothing to become a customer, and it requires no special equipment.

MCI is another privately operated long distance firm joining in the competition with Bell. Others will be joining the ranks in the near future.

TELEGRAM
Use of the telegram in the United States has been on the decline in recent years because telephone service has proven more practical and effective while telegraph service has become increasingly inefficient. In the U.S. the telegram is primarily used when a communi-

cation must be in writing and speed is essential. In the case of foreign telegrams (cables), the cost is fairly high but still cheaper than the telephone for short messages. And since average citizens don't have a telex console at their disposal, a cable or telegram might be the only alternative to making an international phone call.

TELEX
This system of teletype communication, not as commonly used in the United States, is very popular in Europe. It is much cheaper than telephone or telegraph and is the preferred method of communication for airlines, hotels, and international business concerns. The message is typed on a teletype machine, while another prints out the message at the receiving end.

TAXES AND ROAD EXPENSE REPORTS

For proper tax deductions it is required that you keep detailed records of deductable expenses while on tour or business trips. The general rules are that any expense over $25 must have a receipt to verify it, showing date, place, amount, and item. And any and all hotel or lodging bills must have a receipt for proof no matter what amount. Lesser items, such as meals and tips, need not have receipts so long as regular reports are filed and so long as they aren't inordinately high.

You might be surprised at the kinds of things a touring musician can deduct. The following is a partial list:

1. Travel and transport: airplane, train, and bus tickets; freight and shipping; excess baggage charges.
2. Auto and taxi: car rental, taxi fares, gas, oil, repairs.
3. Meals and lodging: hotel and motel bills, meal costs, tips.
4. Public relations: food and/or drinks for business contacts, such as disc jockeys, promoters, members of the press, interviewers, fans.
5. Promotional press material, press kits, photos, advertising expenses.
6. Music supplies: repairs, accessories, music, records, tapes, rehearsal rental time.
7. Music equipment (depreciated over the years): instruments, cases, sound equipment, hi-fi equipment (for research and study).
8. Postage and stationery: mailing costs, stationery supplies.

9. Laundry and cleaning (of performing outfits).
10. Telephone and telegram (for business of course).

On a tour-by-tour, monthly, or yearly basis, the road expense reports are compiled as part of the income tax report you will have to file each year. (See sample daily cash disbursement form and Road Manager Expense Record in Appendix B.) To keep these notations, some travelers use a diary book, and except for the possibility of losing the entire thing toward the middle of the year, this is a good method. My preference is to keep individual sheets for each day's report to which the appropriate receipts can be attached.

CARNET APPLICATIONS

If you are planning a European tour, you may need a carnet form to register your equipment (a complete list of countries requiring carnets is found in Appendix E.) This registration guarantees the countries you visit that you will be returning to the U.S. with your possessions and not selling them abroad. All the equipment listed on a carnet must travel together across borders and eventually return together. If you expect to divide your equipment for separate trips in a tour, then apply for separate carnets. (See Appendix E for particulars, addresses, and phone number.)

Instead of being handled by the government as it is in many other countries, the U.S. Chamber of Commerce administrates the Carnet Bureau in this country. This is a nonprofit organization run by large multinational corporations. Unfortunately it's a losing proposition for the American needing a carnet. The fees are ridiculously high ($50 and up for each carnet) compared with other countries where there is no fee at all or a token charge. Also unfortunately, this is a bureaucracy, true to its definition and not the easiest or most reliable office to deal with. Upon request they will send you information and application forms. Allow one month, if possible, before your tour to apply for carnets—the wheels do turn slowly.

Certain countries are very strict, demanding a carnet for any instrument not small enough to carry as hand baggage. These are England, France, Norway, and the Eastern European countries including Yugoslavia.

The carnet bureau application will require your particulars and request three important things: (1) How many countries you will visit. (How many times you will cross borders, even if it's between the same countries several times.) (2) The number of transits. (How many times you will travel through a country without performing. Plane connections don't count unless you leave the customs area.) (3) The date you intend to depart the U.S. (I always give it a week or two early to make sure they send the forms in time. Also if anything is incorrect, I would want the time to correct it. My last carnet arrived without enough sheets despite my requesting the right amount. When I called, the woman I spoke with said they had "presumed" that I didn't need as many as I had asked for. This kind of attitude is to be expected, so be prepared.)

You will be asked to place a value on the equipment for the purpose of setting a security deposit and fee. I suggest you make the value as low as reasonably possible to keep your deposit small. Almost always your instruments will be used and the value an arbitrary thing, so a set of drums could be valued at $200 or $300, an amp at $150, etc.

The deposit is 40 percent of the value and the carnet fee is also based on equipment value. Up to $499.99 the fee is $50; from $500 to $4,999.99 the fee is $75; from $5,000 to $9,999.99 it is $100; from $10,000 to $19,999.99, $125; and over $20,000 the fee is $150. A cashier's check is the only reasonable form of payment the bureau will accept to cover both fee and deposit. (A bank letter of credit or bond is also acceptable for the deposit, but these items are difficult to obtain and very expensive. At least when you make a cash deposit yourself, you get the full amount in refund when you turn in the carnet at the end of the tour.) Enclose the payrnent and deposit checks with your application.

The deposit is returned after the expiration (30 months) or when you send the carnet form back for cancellation at the end of your tour. *Be sure to keep the form number for reference, as well as the receipt from your cashier's check, in case of any difficulty in getting your deposit refunded.*

In addition to the application form, you will compile a general list describing the equipment, listing the serial numbers, brand names, approximate weight, value, and country of origin.

When your carnet arrives, look to see if there is a set of two pages for each country you will visit. The white pages are for the countries you will perform in, blue are for passing through, and yellow for country of departure at the beginning of the tour.

Next, take your equipment to a U.S. customs office such as the airport customs when you depart. The officer will fill in the first yellow sheet and—*most important—will stamp the first sheet and cover of the carnet to make it valid.* Some officers are not so experienced with carnet forms, so be sure the front does get stamped. Each time you enter a country you will fill in certain information on each sheet at customs, giving your name, purpose, and brief description of the equipment. They will fill in the import sheet and stamp it; when you leave, the export sheet gets the attention. And each time the customs officer will tear off part for their records. A few countries are now charging a fee to process a carnet at their border. Switzerland sometimes charges 12 francs (about $8) per carnet, but most don't charge for this service.

Do not skip customs or you may have problems. Not all countries are strict about requiring a carnet, but those which are (France, Great Britain, Norway, Yugoslavia) will not like it if you have not been keeping the carnet up to date. Be forewarned that customs offices are sometimes closed for the lunch hour and perhaps at any time at minor border crossings as well as at night and weekends. So try to stick to major routes for the handling of carnets because lesser crossings might not have the facilities. You also may have trouble using a carnet on the train. While crossing a border, customs officers are on board checking your personal papers but are not always equipped or authorized to check equipment and fill out carnets.

TIP

If you use a carnet when entering a country, make certain to use the exit form when you leave the country, or there will be a delay on getting your deposit money back at the end of the tour.

At the end of the tour, U.S. customs will fill in the remaining yellow sheet verifying that you have returned with all that is listed. At this point you can mail the form back to the bureau to get your deposit refunded. If you lose the carnet or fail to return with the equipment, you will most likely forfeit your deposit or at least part of it.

My personal observation is that the equipment is rarely checked for serial numbers by either U.S. or foreign customs. But I still advise sticking to the rules lest the occasional zealot is lurking about, waiting to see that *everything* is accounted for. It's a troublesome nuisance on European tours to have to mess with a carnet, but face it, it's usually necessary. Several bands have been denied entry to some countries lately because they had equipment with no carnet; it's just not worth the risk of missing concerts.

TIP

Always keep carnets safely so that you have access to them at all times. Don't pack them in your luggage, for instance. A lost one would create a mess.

MUSICIANS' UNION

Getting all the facts straight on the Musicians' Union is no easy matter. This is partly because procedures vary from local to local, but more so because a lot of the rules are not followed to the letter.

There are a few general points to know, however. Being a member in *any* local permits you to play traveling engagements (stays of two weeks or less) and recording sessions anywhere in the U.S. and Canada. Unless you expect to work steadily in cities where membership costs are high, it is much more economical to be a member of a small town local. If you live or grew up in a small town, then joining and keeping your membership there could be practical. When you transfer or join a large city local, there is usually a waiting period of three to six months during which you forfeit your previous card and are allowed to play only nonsteady engagements.

Some union locals offer extra benefits beyond the areas of setting salary rates and standing behind union contracts. These might include life insurance policies, low-cost group health insurance plans, recreational facilities, credit unions, rehearsal halls, etc.

In the major centers for the recording industry, union locals will collect the paycheck for members from the record company and disperse them through the local office (coincidentally guaranteeing that you pay the work dues).

When booking an engagement, the union contract is the standard form for the agreement between musician and promoter. (See sample in Appendix D.) The union rules call for a copy to be sent to the local that has jurisdiction over the job in advance of the engagement. The union will then bill you for work dues—a small amount, really—or send a representative around to collect personally. Many, perhaps even most, locals don't get upset if the contract is not filed in advance. So many groups don't do this on every engagement. Mostly it is the larger city locals which are particular, like those in New York City, Philadelphia, Chicago, and Honolulu, for instance. If you haven't filed and you get approached by a union agent at a concert, at least be able to offer a copy of the contract on the spot and apologize for failing to file a contract in advance. At the very least, have an explanation to the effect that the booking was made at the last minute, that the conract was held up and just got returned, or something to justify the failure to send in the contract ahead. If you have a copy with you and are gracious about it, that's usually as far as it goes.

If you get a letter stating that the union local is bringing you up on charges for not filing a contract on a gig (this has happened to me once in 15 years), write an apology making what excuses you can. This may end the matter for you, or at the worst, be prepared for the small fine.

Don't expect the union to be a big help if you are having trouble collecting performance money. In case of flagrant offenders, the union will put them on the unfair list. But in minor cases, the union will often be better friends with the club owner or promoter located in the area than with a band traveling through, usually giving him every benefit of doubt and invoking every possible technicality to let him off the hook.

My own theory is don't expect too much from the union and you won't be disappointed. Stay out of the way and you won't have trouble. Not a great vote of approval, I realize.

CHAPTER 6

CREDIT, LOANS, AND INSURANCE FOR MUSICIANS (AND OTHER UNSAVORY CHARACTERS)

CREDIT RATING

As early in your career as possible, try to establish a good credit rating. Ironically, you can go through life paying for all your needs in cash and then find when you really need to borrow money desperately, you don't have a credit rating permitting you to do so. Since the definition of a good credit rating is a history of borrowing and repaying on time, it makes good sense to start buying occasionally on the installment plan or making small bank loans as soon as possible. This will greatly enhance your ability to obtain a credit card, mortgage, or emergency loan.

Your first loan may have to be guaranteed by a cosigner—a signer who has already established a good credit rating and who will agree to take over the loan if you fail to make payment. Good prospects would be a relative, manager, or agent if you're on close terms. But remember what a tremendous favor this is, considering, according to banks, the high incidence of failure to pay on cosigner notes.

Another good way to establish credit is to borrow against a savings account. If you have a decent-sized savings account, take out a loan for a modest amount—say, $500—and use your $500 in savings as collateral. The bank will hold the $500 until you pay the loan back over a period of six months to a year. You'll have to pay interest of course, but this is a small price to pay for starting a good payment history.

If, over a period of several years, you have established your credibility, you'll be able to borrow any time you need to. There are a number of major acquisitions, such as a house, car, or college education, almost impossible to buy with cash, so it is of great importance, particularly for a musician, to have a solid credit rating established.

CREDIT UNIONS

Similar to banks in that you are paid interest on your savings and can borrow money, credit unions are another good way for people in "usually unreliable" professions to establish credit. Some musicians' unions, like the one in New York City, have a credit union for members. If you become a saver at their credit union, after a period of time you are then eligible to take out loans, and the interest rates are more favorable.

AUTO LOANS

Probably one of the easiest types of loans to obtain is the auto loan. Not only is this a common installment purchase item, but there is always the car to use as collateral. The car dealer will be able to suggest the bank it deals with or you can try your own. Or some auto companies have their own credit agencies. Most people will find the greatest cooperation from their own bank, particularly if you have a good record of doing business with them.

If you lack steady employment or the financial status the bank finds necessary, then your next option is to use a cosigner. There isn't really much risk in this since the car can be sold to end the indebtedness.

An auto loan is frequently the first type of loan anyone encounters and is an excellent point to begin a solid credit rating. If someone cosigns your first loan they are doing you the double favor of helping you establish your credit as well as securing the property you want.

AUTO INSURANCE

There are certain professions which many insurance companies consider unacceptable on almost any terms. Unfortunately, these include musicians. The image of the drunken, irresponsible musician driving a band all over the country is apparently the one that comes first to the insurance agent's mind.

Auto insurance is primarily intended to cover the owner of the car, so that a driver other than the owner should be fully authorized, meet age requirements, and be acting as an employee conducting business for the car owner in order to be fully covered. Law requires the proof of ownership, registration, and insurance be present in the car. Also if someone other than the owner is driving the car, a letter of authorization from him will eliminate such inconveniences, for one, as being charged with car theft during an out-of-state inquiry. A reminder: if you are using the car in an illegal way (while intoxicated or unlicensed driver, carrying narcotics, etc.) and are in an accident, your insurance may be invalidated or limited, and you could be liable for personal injury claims for very high amounts.

I've had some insurance agents come right out and tell me I would have to put something other than musician on the application to be even considered for approval. Since the insurance agent is just a salesperson trying to make a deal between you and the company, he'll be on your side for the most part because he wants to make a sale. Of course, if he thinks you're a bad risk, he'll discourage you himself, but if you make a favorable impression as a responsible person, you can count on his assistance.

TIP

Musicians are notoriously poor insurance risks and are frequently refused upon first mention of this occupation. It might be wise to stress other credentials. Perhaps you have other, part-time employment of a more reputable nature or a family connection to back you up. Try to avoid coming right out with the information that you might be planning to drive a load of weird musicians all over the country or you will surely find insurance hard to come by. Also if one company checks you out and finds you wanting, they usually circulate this information, so make your first shot your best one.

The insurance company will most likely not investigate your source of employment before approving the application, so don't worry about stretching the truth a little. If you have any other part-time work or affiliation, use that as a reference. Use employment from the past, if it comes to that, or say you are a publisher if you have published any tunes, a teacher if you have taught—anything but admitting to "full-time musician." You can be temporarily laid off; they don't care so long as you can pay the premium. Also if you have any relatives or business associates who can act as a reference for you with their insurance agencies, that will go a long way toward smoothing the process.

It is hard to weigh the differences between companies. Rates may vary, though some states set specific rates. Ask the agent, who may in fact be acting for more than one company, if he knows of any remarkable practices, such as the canceling of insurance after only one accident, by a company you would want to avoid. One thing is a fact: insurance companies keep each other's computers informed of anyone who has been turned down for auto coverage or who is a bad risk, so beware of applying in a careless way.

Various factors go into a company's decision to accept you and set the rate they'll charge: if you are under 21, it's a high-risk consideration; under 25, still high but not as bad; single or married; homeowner or renter; kind of neighborhood you live in; and, of course, your profession; all are considered. Also any previous accidents or traffic violations may be taken into account. Some states, Massachusetts, for one, have done away with most of these discriminating criteria for setting rates.

I recommend carrying rather full protection. The minimum required in most states is not really adequate to protect you in any major accident. If your auto is not an old junker, but actually worth something, you'll want to have collision for the protection of your investment. If you expect to be carrying other musicians to jobs, driving on long trips, or frequently roving out of state, you'll probably want to be heavily insured. Remember, in case of an accident, you can be sued for injury cost to victims and property damage to other cars or property. Your whole life could be drastically changed for the worse, even if you suffered no injury yourself, due to inadequate coverage.

TIP

Bear in mind that if you do anything to invalidate your coverage, you are taking a great risk. This includes failing to properly register your car, neglecting insurance payments, drinking, having drugs in the car, or any illegal activity. Don't let anyone take the wheel who is unlicensed or younger than your insurance permits. Also be aware that having an open bottle of alcoholic beverage in the car is illegal and could invalidate your insurance in an accident.

The premium can be paid on the installment plan, although you save an interest charge if you can pay in full.

TRAVEL INSURANCE

An easily acquired, inexpensive insurance is travel accident. You will be covered for accident to your person during any form of travel. For loss of life, a full benefit (say, $10,000 to $100,000) is paid to your beneficiary. For major injuries, a partial payment is made to you. Any insurance agent can fix you up with a policy.

American Express and Diner's Club automatically include $75,000 flight accident insurance if you purchase a ticket on their credit card. Low-cost group rate travel insurance is offered Airline Passenger Association members and through the American Automobile Association.

Accident coverage that includes all travel, not just on airplanes, is perhaps more sensible and this is available through the Automobile Association of America, and various insurance companies. Separately purchased flight insurance for each flight is rather overpriced and not considered a fair bargain by most experts.

TIP

Always carry proof of insurance, registration and/or proof of ownership in the car at all times.

If someone other than the owner is driving the car without the owner, there should be a letter of authorization from the owner so the driver won't be suspected of theft in the event of police intervention.

Also, drivers other than the owner should be listed on the insurance policy for your own protection to avoid problems later in case of an accident.

PERSONAL PROPERTY INSURANCE

You can get insurance against your instruments being stolen from your house or apartment in most areas of the country, but coverage while on the road is just about impossible. A personal property policy on a house or property might cover instruments as long as their value isn't extremely high, but don't count on it.

If you are the fortunate owner of thousands of dollars worth of instruments and sound equipment, you'll have to take out a separate "floater" policy, as it's called, which lists one by one the items and their values. Coverage is still limited to theft from your residence, but the price is not outrageously high.

The more insurance you carry with an agency the more agreeable they will be to fill your additional insurance needs. If you already have auto insurance and homeowner's, then the floater policy is no problem. It is extremely difficult to get insurance for your possessions if you live in an apartment, especially if this is in a high crime area or large city. Try anyway.

TIP

As a personal precaution, keep a list of equipment serial numbers, and purchase receipts to verify value in case of theft. It also helps to mark each piece with an engraving tool or indelible mark—use your social security number.

When shipping equipment by any form of commercial transport, it is possible to take out inexpensive insurance to protect against loss or damage during shipment. (See Loss or Damage in Chapter 2.)

HEALTH INSURANCE

Any traveling musician would be well advised to have a nationally recognized form of health insurance. In case of accident or sudden illness, you might find yourself taken to a hospital *anywhere*. Many hospitals are reluctant to admit anyone without identification of health insurance, and there are always horror stories of severely injured people having treatment delayed because their financial condition is uncertain. With medical costs as overwhelming as they are today, it's too great a risk to go without at least *some* insurance.

Some musicians' unions, such as the one in New York City, have group insurance plans which substantially reduce the cost of necessary health coverage.

AFTERWORD

I hope the material in this book proves helpful and that the information will make your travel more comfortable and your road life more bearable. For all its negative aspects, road life comes with both a grand tradition and a certain inevitable contact with the realities of life which one can miss living in one spot on the planet.

There's something about having dinner at a gourmet restaurant and then being happy to follow that with a snack cake and soft drink at an all-night filling station for your next meal, that gives you a certain perspective on the variations of life in this modern world. Without a doubt, road life will never be routine, and is seldom dull.

APPENDIXES

APPENDIX A
CHECKLISTS

AT LEAST TWO WEEKS BEFORE TOUR:

1. Make certain that all contracts are complete, signed, and in hand. Read over details, note times, number of shows, form of payment, etc.

2. Have itinerary list with promoters' names and addresses, hotel information, flight schedules, and concert hall information prepared for musicians and personnel.

3. Get together expense report forms for use on the road.

4. Check to see that advance deposits have been received. Arrange for cash payments as needed during the tour.

5. Make hotel reservations and obtain written confirmation of them.

6. Be sure that all airline reservations are made as needed, confirmed, and that tickets are in hand.

7. Make rental car reservations, if needed.

8. Compute and allow for sufficient travel funds.

9. Maps and locations of concert halls and hotels and hard-to-find locations should be obtained from promoters.

10. Arrange to be met on arrival, if needed.

11. Check on equipment to be furnished by local promoters.

12. Check on equipment to be brought on tour (cases in good condition for travel, equipment in good repair, everything accounted for).

13. Prepare list of serial numbers and description of all equipment going on tour in case of theft. You won't be able to help the police, nor will they be able to help you, if you can't identify your instruments.

14. Speak to promoter or representative to confirm details (time of arrival in town and at hotel, time of soundcheck, performance times, other groups on the bill, equipment and staging requirements, security, parking, your guest passes and refreshments, etc.) Note: performance times frequently are changed after the contract

is written up, so always ask to make certain you know the correct plan. Plus, many promoters ignore contract requirements unless specifically reminded—they can provide almost anything if given time to get it together.

15. Send copy of the contract to union local of the concert site if expected to do so.

16. Check on weather conditions, if winter time.

FOREIGN TOURS:

17. Apply for necessary visas (check with promoters, check with Consulate of the countries in question, allow as much time as possible for this since it can take as long as several weeks).

18. Check to see that everyone's passport is up to date, and that there are enough blank pages left in the passports.

19. Get necessary electric plug adapters, transformers, converters, etc.

DAY BEFORE TOUR:

1. Reconfirm reservations: airplane, cars, hotels, etc. unless you already have written confirmations on hand. Let the airlines know if you have any special requirements like mountains of excess baggage. Notify the hotel if you're expecting an irregular arrival time.

2. Make sure all contracts are completed and on hand. Check to see that the riders are signed.

3. Make sure all advance deposits are in.

4. Check on local weather conditions, especially if driving. To get local weather along your route, try calling the state police, local weather bureaus, or the auto club.

5. Get directions for finding hotels, concert halls if traveling by your own means.

6. Call promoter, if necessary, to check on any last minute details.

7. Check travel plans and departure times with all musicians and personnel.

8. Have all tickets in hand, and proofread for possible errors.

FOREIGN TOURS:

9. Upon departure from U.S., have carnet validated at U.S. Customs office in airport or at border crossing.

TO TAKE ALONG:

1. List of equipment serial numbers
2. Contracts
3. Itineraries
4. Copies of reservations
5. Tickets
6. Cash for expenses
7. Credit cards, if you use them
8. Tape (gray, duct tape for stage set-up and repairs)
9. Spare parts for equipment
10. Stamps and envelopes
11. Tax record expense forms
12. Phone numbers of all necessary contacts
13. Baggage tags
14. Scotch tape, glue, needle, and thread

FOREIGN TOURS:

15. Plug adapters, transformers
16. Carnets
17. Passports and visas

WHEN YOU ARRIVE AT CONCERT:

1. Check hall for stage set-up, lighting, sound, and seating, so if any adjustments are necessary, there will be time to get them done.

2. Check dressing rooms for cleanliness, security, necessary facilities, towels, water, refreshments, etc.

3. Check on parking, unloading, and vehicle security.

4. Check times for set-up, soundcheck, performance.

5. Make a friendly contact with the stage manager, especially if the stage hands are union, for they are often reluctant to let anyone assist in the movement or set-up of equipment and a good rapport won't hurt.

6. Allow time for eating and rest—things will go smoother.

7. Go over guest list and backstage security procedures.

8. Check on box office if applicable (percentage engagement).

9. Verify form of payment and when it will be transacted. A good time to accept payment is before the last set or only show. Remember, if there is any question, you have some bargaining power *before* your performance.

FOREIGN TOURS:

10. Check on travel plans for following day, ground transportation, reconfirmation of air reservations, etc.

AFTER THE GIG:

1. Verify plans for the overnight security of the equipment. If your paraphernalia is too cumbersome to take into the hotel room, a possible alternative is to leave it locked in the hall until the next day.

2. Fill out the daily expense report, attaching all receipts and notations.

3. Make sure wake-up is arranged for everyone if an early morning departure is expected the next day. If you are dependent on a local host for transportation or for keeping your equipment overnight, be sure to have his phone number ready in case he oversleeps. In fact, local promoters are notorious for late night celebrations after the concert, so early next morning they might not be as reliable as the night before.

HOTEL CHECK-IN:

1. One person check-in for all, if possible, mention first the reservations, dates, and number of rooms.

2. Know when reservations were made and by whom in case of confusion at front desk.

3. Pay in advance in cash, or use credit card for reference when checking in. (Use pre-registration list when checking-in in large

groups.) Specify who pays extra charges, who pays room charge, check on rate charged for rooms, mention any special requirements, (access for easy loading, types of beds, etc.).

4. Give name list with assigned room number to hotel, and ask for it to be given immediately to the hotel telephone operator.

5. Give similar copy of room list to each member of the group for reference.

6. Give keys to appropriate people.

7. Get bell-hop to assist with baggage if needed and tip accordingly.

8. Park cars.

HOTEL CHECK-OUT:
1. Check out an hour or so before departure time.

2. Make sure extras are paid by appropriate persons.

3. Check receipts for mistakes or erroneous charges.

4. Save receipts.

5. Arrange for baggage to be picked up from rooms by bellhop.

6. Have cars brought to hotel entrance.

SUPPLY KIT FOR CAR:
1. Pliers, screwdrivers, wrenches

2. Battery booster cables

3. Rags

4. Wire for minor repairs

5. Tape

6. Spare fuses, bulbs

7. Tire gauge

8. Shovel (if winter)

9. Road atlas

10. Disto-map

11. Proof of insurance

12. Registration, proof of ownership

APPENDIX B
SAMPLES OF TOURING FORMS

ITINERARY

AUGUST 23

Travel: depart New York, LaGuardia
9:40 A.M. American Airlines #402
arrive Chicago 11:30 A.M.

Hotel: Holiday Inn
2002 Winchester Ave.
Glen Falls, Ill. 60534
(312) 354-6464
6 single rooms for 1 night

Location: Music Hall Theatre
2400 Croydon Road
Chicago, Ill. 60752
(312) 466-5352

Contact: Phil Payton
Don Gray (stage manager)

Sound check: 4:30

Performance time: 8:00 (doors open at 6:30)

Additional information: Radio interview scheduled for 7:00, in dressing room at hall, WSOC-FM, DJ Randy Sawyer.

AUGUST 24

Depart hotel at 10:00 A.M.

Travel: depart in rental cars at 10:15 A.M. for Kalamazoo
arrive Kalamazoo at 1:00 P.M.

Hotel: Kalamazoo Sheraton
1302 Second St.
Kalamazoo, Mich. 30045
(203) 243-1213
6 singles   1 night

Location: U. of Michigan (outdoors)
            Campus Road
            Parade grounds

Contact: Ron Sandy
            (203) 344-5789

Performance time: 4:00

Sound check: 2:00

Additional information: opening act begins at 3:00, party after the concert at residence hall with press interviews, stay one hour, back to hotel by 6:30.

AUGUST 26

Equipment depart by truck in early morning

Depart hotel at 11:00 A.M.

Travel: depart Kalamazoo Airport 12:30 P.M. United #345
          arrive Cleveland 2:05 P.M.

Hotel: Holiday Inn
         242 Water St.
         Cleveland, Ohio 95846
         (416) 566-7543
         6 singles   1 night

Location: University of Ohio
            Fairlawn Hall
            2400 Banks St.
            Cleveland

Contact: John Metner
           255-6790

Sound check: 4:00

Performance: 8:00

DAILY CASH DISBURSEMENT REPORT

ENGAGEMENT _____ DATE _____
              Name   Place

Transport and travel _____

Autos and taxis _____

Meals and lodging _____

Music: supplies, special materials, rehearsals _____

Promotion, entertainment _____

Stagehands, technicians _____

Public relations _____

Telephone and telegraph _____

Uniforms, laundry, cleaning _____

Union, taxes _____

Stationery, printing, postage _____

ROAD MANAGER EXPENSE RECORD

Period ending_____

Date	Receipt No.	PAID TO	FOR	Amount Cash	Charge

Submitted by: _____ Date_____ TOTAL

Submit in duplicate with receipts   Page____of____Pages

PERSONAL INFORMATION

1. Name and address: _____
   _____
   _____

2. Passport number, date of issue, etc.: _____
   _____

3. Credit cards, numbers: _____
   _____
   _____
   _____
   _____

4. Insurance agents, policies: _____
   _____
   _____

5. Bank account numbers: _____
   _____

6. Touring equipment serial numbers: _____
   _____

7. Doctor, dentist, lawyer: _____
   _____

HOTEL RESERVATION CONFIRMATION LETTER

HOTEL NAME

Address

    Attention: RESERVATIONS

Dear Sirs:

    This is to confirm reservations for _____ (single and/or double) rooms at your hotel, at a rate of $_____/room for the night(s) of _____. These reservations were made by _____ by phone [or whichever applies] through your reservations office in _____.

    Following is a list of the people who are in the group: [List *all* names, road manager first.] Mr. _____ (road manager's name) is our representative and will assist you in any way possible. In the event that you can pre-register the group, this would be a welcome convenience for Mr. _____.

APPENDIX C
USEFUL BOOKS AND ADDRESSES

REFERENCE MATERIALS

Official Airline Guide. Available from the address given below.

OAG Travel Planner, Hotel/Motel Guide. Available from A.P.A.; address given below.

Rand McNally Road Atlas of U.S.A. Available in most bookstores.

Disto-Map. Available in bookstores and some filling stations.

Grosse Shell Atlas (Europe). Available in Germany.

Michelin Guide Books (European countries). Available in most bookstores.

Egon Roney Guide Book (hotels in Great Britain). Available in Great Britain.

Toll-Free Digest (of area code 800 numbers). Available in most bookstores, published by Warner Books.

Hotel chain booklets (Holiday Inn, Howard Johnson, Ramada Inn, Sheraton, etc.). Call your local branch or the chain's 800 number for booklets.

ADDRESSES

Official Airline Guide
2000 Clearwater Drive
Oak Brook, Illinois 60521
(800) 323-3537

Airline Passengers Association
P.O. Box 2758
Dallas, Texas 75221

Automobile Association
of America
(AAA) National Headquarters
8111 Gatehouse Road
Falls Church, Virginia 22047
(703) AAA-6601
(Check local listing for your city.)

For information on the
Eurail Guide, write:
French National Railroads
610 Fifth Avenue
New York, New York 10017
(212) 949-0400

Southern Pacific Communications
P.O. Box 974
Burlingame, California 94010

APPENDIX D
SAMPLE CONTRACTS

CONTRACT BLANK

This contract for the personal services of musicians on the engagement described below, made this _____ day of _____, 19____ between the undersigned Purchaser of Music (herein called "Employer") and _____ musicians (including leader). The musicians are engaged severally on the terms and conditions on the face hereof. The leader represents that the musicians already designated have agreed to be bound by said terms and conditions. Each musician yet to be chosen, upon acceptance, shall be bound by said terms and conditions. Each musician may enforce this agreement. The musicians severally agree to render services under the undersigned leader.

1. Name and Address of Place of Engagement _____

_____

Name of Band or Group _____

2. Date(s), starting and finishing time of engagement _____

_____

3. Type of Engagement _____

_____

4. Wage agreed upon $ _____
This wage includes expenses agreed to be reimbursed by the employer in accordance with the attached schedule, or a schedule to be furnished the Employer on or before the date of the engagement.

5. Employer will make payments as follows: _____

_____

_____

Upon request by the Federation or the local in whose jurisdiction the musicians shall perform hereunder, Employer either shall make advance payment hereunder or shall post an appropriate bond.

If the engagement is subject to contribution to the A.F.M. & E.P.W. Pension Welfare Fund, the leader will collect same from the Employer and pay it to the Fund; and the Employer and leader agree to be bound by the Trust Indenture dated October 2, 1959, as amended, relating to services rendered hereunder in the U.S., and by the Agreement and Declaration of Trust dated April 9, 1962, as amended, relating to services rendered hereunder in Canada.

6. The Employer shall at all times have complete supervision, direction and control over the services of musicians on this engagement and expressly reserves the right to control the manner, means and details of the performance of services by the musicians including the leader as well as the ends to be accomplished. If any musicians have not been chosen upon the signing of this contract, the leader shall, as agent for the Employer and under his instructions, hire such persons and any replacements as are required.

7. In accordance with the Constitution, By-laws, Rules and Regulations of the Federation, the parties will submit every claim, dispute, controversy or difference involving the musical services arising out of or connected with this contract and the engagement covered thereby for determination by the International Executive Board of the Federation of a similar board of an appropriate local thereof and such determination shall be conclusive, final and binding upon the parties.

ADDITIONAL TERMS AND CONDITIONS

The leader shall, as agent of the employer, enforce disciplinary measures for just cause, and carry out instructions as to selections and manner of performance. The agreement of the musicians to perform is subject to proven detention by sickness, accidents, riots, strikes, acts of God, or any other legitimate conditions beyond their control. On behalf of the Employer the leader will distribute the amount received from the Employer to the musicians, including himself as indicated on the opposite side of this contract, or in place thereof from each musician, including himself. The amount paid to the leader includes the cost of transportation, which will be reported by the leader to the Employer.

All employees covered by this agreement must be members in good standing of the Federation. However, if the employment provided for hereunder is subject to the Labor-Management Relations Act, 1947, all employees who are members of the Federation when their employment commences hereunder shall be continued in such employment only so long as they continue such membership in good standing. All other employees covered by this agreement, on or before the thirtieth day following the commencement of their employment, or the effective date of this agreement, whichever is later, shall become and continue to be members in good standing of the Federation. The provisions of this paragraph shall not become effective unless and until permitted by applicable law.

To the extent permitted by applicable law, nothing in this contract shall ever be construed so as to interfere with any duty owing by any musician performing hereunder to the Federation pursuant to its Constitution, By-laws, Rules, Regulations, and Orders.

Any musicians on this engagement are free to cease service hereunder by reason of any strike, ban, unfair list order or requirement of the Federation or of any Federation local approved by the Federation or by any reason of any other labor dispute approved by the Federation, and shall be free to accept and engage in other employment of the same or similar character or otherwise, without any restraint, hindrance, penalty, obligation or liability whatever, any other provisions of this contract to the contrary notwithstanding.

Representatives of the Federation local in whose jurisdiction the musicians shall perform hereunder shall have access to the place of performance (except to private residences) for the purpose of conferring with the musicians.

No performance on the engagement shall be recorded, reproduced or transmitted from the place of performance, in any manner or by any means whatsoever, in the absence of a specific written agreement with the Federation relating to and permitting such a recording, reproduction, or transmission.

The Employer represents that there does not exist against him, in favor of any member of the Federation, any claim of any kind arising out of musical services rendered for such Employer. No musician will be required to perform any provisions of this contract or to render any services for said Employer as long as such claim is unsatisfied or unpaid, in whole or in part. If Employer breaches this agreement he shall pay the musicians in addition to damages, 6% interest thereon plus a reasonable attorney's fee.

To the extent permitted by applicable law, all of the Constitution, By-laws, Rules and Regulations of the Federation and of any local thereof applicable to this engagement (not in conflict with those of the Federation) will be adhered to and the parties acknowledge that they are and each has the obligation to be, fully acquainted therewith.

—SEE ANY ATTACHED RIDERS—

Employer's Name	Leader's Name Local no.
Signature of Employer	Signature of Leader
Address	Address
City State Zip	City State Zip
Telephone	Booking Agent Agreement no.

This contract does not conclusively determine the person liable to report and pay employment taxes and similar levies under rulings of the U.S. Internal Revenue Service and of some state agencies.

CONTRACT RIDER

THIS RIDER IS HEREWITH ATTACHED TO AND MADE PART OF THE CONTRACT DATED _____ BY AND BE-TWEEN _____, HEREINAFTER REFERRED TO AS THE PRODUCER, AND _____
_____HEREIN-AFTER REFERRED TO AS THE PURCHASER, FOR THE SERVICES OF _____.

PLEASE READ THIS RIDER CAREFULLY. IT CONTAINS A DESCRIPTION OF CERTAIN EQUIPMENT REQUIREMENTS AND VARIOUS WORKING CONDITIONS ESSENTIAL TO THE PRODUCER AND NECESSARY FOR THE HIGHEST QUALITY PERFORMANCE. YOU SHOULD CALL OUR AGENT OR MANAGEMENT IF YOU HAVE ANY QUESTIONS ABOUT THIS RIDER OR IF THERE ARE CERTAIN TERMS OR CONDITIONS WHICH YOU ANTICIPATE HAVING TROUBLE ARRANGING. BY SIGNING THIS RIDER YOU ARE AGREEING TO FULFILL ALL THE REQUIREMENTS LISTED. ANY BREACH OF THE TERMS OF THIS RIDER WILL CONSTITUTE A BREACH OF THE ATTACHED CONTRACT.

EQUIPMENT, PRODUCTION AND STAGING REQUIREMENTS

A. Purchaser agrees to provide for the Producer, at Purchaser's sole cost and expense:

A1. One nine foot concert grand piano of a quality and condition meeting the Producer's standards as verified by the Producer's representative. The selection and rental of the piano is subject to consultation with Producer's representative and must be arranged and approved by Producer's representative.

A2. Piano should be delivered and positioned on performance stage at least six hours before concert is scheduled to begin. Temperature, humidity and lighting on stage should, at the time of piano delivery, be adjusted to most resemble conditions that will exist during concert and thus minimize the changes in the piano strings, hammers, wood frame, springs and other parts which sometimes are affected by changing atmospheric conditions.

A3. Piano must be tuned to A440 pitch on the day of performance and immediately prior to the Producer's arrival at the performance site. Tuning must occur after the piano is positioned on stage at its final performance position and cannot be moved after tuning takes place.

A4. Piano tuner must be present at the performance site at the scheduled time of arrival of the Producer so he can be advised by Producer as to what additional adjustments and retunings are necessary. Piano tuner must be available at all times while Producer is at performance site during "sound check" and MUST STAY AND RETUNE THE PIANO DURING INTERMISSION, AFTER WHICH, HE WILL BE DISMISSED.

A5. Producer shall have sole and exclusive control over the production, presentation and performance of its portion of the engagement hereunder.

A6. A stage area forty (40) feet wide and twenty-five (25) feet deep for the exclusive use of the Producer. Purchaser agrees that this stage will be kept free of people and equipment during the time that it is assigned to Producer. Purchaser further agrees that if the engagement is to be outdoors there will be a covering over the stage that will protect Artists and equipment from the elements to the Producer's satisfaction. In the event that it is necessary for the Purchaser to have other artists, their employees and equipment on this stage during the time assigned to the Producer, Purchaser agrees that they will not occupy the space allocated to Producer, and that their presence will be concealed from the audience by means of curtains, drops and screens.

A7. Adequate electrical service and electrical facilities to be installed by licensed electricians, who will be on hand, and professional personnel in accordance with the standards of community for the installation and operation in a safe manner for electrical appliances, for 300 AMP service, either single phase, 3 wire, or 3 phase, 4 wire within 50 feet of either side of the performance area. If the building is not capable of this power, something must be provided (e.g., a generator). Otherwise, the entire show cannot go on. The Purchaser is responsible to supply the above.

A8. Access to place of performance for unloading equipment. Producer must be supplied with a minimum of two (2) stage crew to assist with load-ins, setting up and break downs. They are to make themselves known and available to Producer's road manager at load-in and break down time. It is the responsibility of the Purchaser to see that this happens.

A9. The place of performance will be completely ready and available to Producer for a sound check at least six (6) hours prior to performance.

A10. It is specifically agreed and understood that a representative of Producer shall have sole and absolute authority in mixing and controlling all sound and light equipment while Producer is performing, including positioning of sound mixing console board, 75 to 100 feet from the stage in the center of the audience, and two (2) consecutive rows of four (4) seats each should be left open to make this possible (eight (8) seats in all). In order to insure the punctual presentation of the performance contracted for hereunder and rapid correction of any problems which may occur, Producer's road manager, sound man, and equipment men shall be supplied with whatever identification and authorization which may be necessary for complete freedom of movement throughout place of performance.

A11. SOUND SYSTEM: Purchaser shall provide at his own expense:
    (a) A first-class professional sound reinforcement system capable of producing a sound pressure level of 95 dB at a distance of ten (10) meters with 180 degree dispersion and a frequency response of no less than plus/or/minus three (3) dB from 70 Hz to 12,000 Hz. This system shall produce a sound pressure level of no less than 85 dB at the furthest point from the stage at the place of performance. NOTE:

There shall be no more than 1% distortion of any component of the system. Due to the nature of Producer's performance it is essential that you avoid "stack" type speaker structures. Altec "Voice of the Theatre"-type enclosures will be sufficient and more visually suitable. These should also be run without the fans operating to reduce ambience.

(b) In venues exceeding a capacity of three thousand seats, Purchaser shall ask the sound contractor to provide graphic equalization adequate for the tuning of the sound system.

(c) *Additional equipment to be a part of the system:*

(1) 175 feet of twelve channel snake (8 channels mic line, 4 channels fold back.) "Foldback" definition: Feeds from board to sound reinforcement.

(2) *Microphones:*
Five (5) on boom-type microphone stands in excellent condition.
Two (2) microphones on straight type stands in excellent condition.
Seven (7) thirty-foot microphone cables.
Two (2) each: Shure SM 58
Five (5) each: Sennheiser 441

NOTE: Purchaser must notify Producer a minimum of one week prior to engagement for the approval of any equipment used other than what is specified herein.

A12. Purchaser will provide at his sole cost and expense a professional stage lighting system with an assortment of bright colored gels. The lighting system desired is best described as a "concert" lighting system as opposed to a "theatrical" system by which we mean that the lighting is to be turned on at the beginning of the set, left alone and untampered with; no dimming and adjusting. Spot lights are a welcome addition to stage lighting if needed to insure an adequately lit stage, but are not necessary if sufficient stage lights are available.

A13. A representative of Producer shall have final approval of staging.

PERMITS, LICENSES AND WORK VISAS

B1. Purchaser shall furnish and provide at his sole cost and expense all necessary permits, licenses and authorizations from any and all government agencies, bureaus and departments Federal, State or local.

B2. Purchaser shall furnish and provide at his sole cost and expense any and all necessary immigration clearances if concert is to be performed outside the U.S.A.

INSTRUCTIONS FOR AUDIENCE AND STAFF

C1. NO PORTION OF THE PERFORMANCE RENDERED HEREUNDER MAY BE BROADCAST, PHOTOGRAPHED, RECORDED, FILMED, TAPED OR EMBODIED IN ANY FORM FOR ANY PURPOSE OR REPRODUCING SUCH PERFORMANCE AND PURCHASER AGREES THAT IT WILL NOT AUTHORIZE ANY SUCH RECORDING WITHOUT PRIOR WRITTEN CONSENT OF THE PRODUCER. PURCHASER WILL DENY ENTRANCE TO ANY PERSONS CARRYING TAPE OR VIDEO RECORDING DEVICES. WITHOUT LIMITING IN ANY WAY THE GENERALITY OF THE FOREGOING PROHIBITION, IT IS UNDERSTOOD TO INCLUDE MEMBERS OF THE AUDIENCE, PRESS AND PURCHASER'S STAFF.

C2. Purchaser shall not allow audience to enter place of performance until such time as technical set-up has been completed. Producer shall complete said set-up at least one hour prior to time of performance, provided that Purchaser makes the place of performance available for said set-up at least six hours prior to the time of performance.

C3. Purchaser agrees not to allow any person to be seated at the concert who arrives late, until the completion of the composition in progress. It is recommended that the Purchaser emphasize in advance to his public that Producer always strictly adheres to the above mentioned policy and we further require that ushers, staff and security be properly advised that this policy will be in operation. Announcements in the hallway and signs at all entranceways of the theatre informing the audience of this seating policy is REQUIRED.

C4. Lights should be dimmed (or whatever method used) starting ten (10) to fifteen (15) minutes before the start of the concert to facilitate audience being seated on time. No background music, taped or otherwise, is to be played before the concert, during intermission or after concert is over.

ADVERTISING, PROMOTION AND PUBLICITY

D1. Producer shall receive 100% star billing in any and all publicity, press releases and paid advertisements, including, without limitations: newspaper ads, posters, flyers, marquees, signs, lobby boards, programs and tickets.

D2. Purchaser agrees that it will not commit Producer to any personal appearances, interviews, or any other type of promotion or appearance without Producer's prior written consent.

D3. Wherein Producer is performing in headline situation Purchaser agrees that the appearance of any act(s) on the same bill with Producer shall be subject to Producer's prior written approval. If this has not been done, or if Purchaser has not received at least verbal agreement directly from Producer's representative, Producer reserves the right to cancel its performance at any time.

D4. The Producer shall have sole and exclusive approval of the souvenir programs and the Purchaser must get the approval from the Producer prior to the engagement. Purchaser agrees that no other program souvenir or photographs, recordings or any other reading materials shall be sold or distributed in connection with this performance without prior approval of the Producer.

D5. Producer shall not be required to appear or perform before any audience which is segregated on the basis of race, color, creed or where physical violence or injury to Producer is likely to occur.

TRAVEL, HOSPITALITY AND DRESSING ROOM REQUIREMENTS

E1. Purchaser to provide one (1) limousine with driver and one (1) van to be available for Producer and staff to and from airport and to and from sound check and concert. The limousine and van should be capable of carrying two large cases containing microphones and tape recorders, two large instrument cases, luggage for five (5) persons and Producer's entourage of five people.

E2. Parking space for two (2) cars in close proximity and with direct access to stage door, for a period commencing six (6) hours prior to performance and for two (2) hours after.

E3. A comfortable and private dressing room, adequate for use by eight (8) persons equipped with towels, ash trays, chairs or sofas; comfortably heated and/or air conditioned and ventilated and lit. This room shall be in easy access to clean lavatories which are supplied with soap, toilet tissue and at least six (6) towels. These lavatories shall be closed to the general public. Purchaser shall be solely responsible for the security of items in the dressing area, and shall keep all unauthorized persons from entering said area by stationing a representative of the Purchaser outside of the dressing room before, during and after the performance.

E4. Food and refreshments should be available in the dressing room. *Hot coffee with cream and sugar and cold Coca Colas are specifically requested by the Producer and should be available at the beginning of the sound check until Producer's departure after the concert.* Also, bottled water, carbonated and uncarbonated, is specifically requested.

E5. Adequate security personnel for the protection of Producer, persons who travel with Producer and personal property of Producer and said persons. Such security personnel will be available during rehearsals (if necessary), performances and for at least one-half hour after performance. One (1) guard for the dressing room is to guard the dressing room during the entire time the room is in use. The Producer's managers shall have sole control of placement of the stage guards.

E6. Stage and backstage shall be cleared of all persons during performance subject to Producer's discretion.

PAYMENT AND LEGAL CONTRACTURAL CLAUSES

F1. All payments by the Purchaser to Producer required to be made under or pursuant to this agreement, shall be made in the form of cash, money order, certified check, cashier's check, or in the case of concerts performed for a university, by a check drawn on a university account. Payment by cashier's check or certified check is requested. Producer may refuse to accept a personal check as fulfillment of any portion of Purchaser's obligation hereunder. If any balance remains to be paid on the fee hereunder at the time the performance commences, such balance shall be paid to Producer's representative prior to or immediately upon commencement of

Producer's performance. In the event that the compensation payable to Producer hereunder is measured in whole or in part by a percentage of receipts, Purchaser shall pay Producer's representative the balance of the guaranteed amount PRIOR to Producer's performance, in one of the forms specified above. Any balance subsequently due on a percentage computation will be paid as soon as practicable after the closing of the box office, and unless extreme circumstances make it impossible, this will be no later than one half hour before the end of the Producer's last performance hereunder. At that time, a ticket printer's manifest and a detailed box office statement will be given to Producer's representative.

F2. All payments shall be made as provided herein. In the event Purchaser fails to make any payment at the time stipulated herein or breaches any other provision of this agreement, Producer shall have the right to withhold performance without prejudice to its rights hereunder.

F3. Purchaser agrees to the following box office and ticket requirements:

    a) Purchaser will provide Producer with maximum of thirty (30) complimentary tickets of the highest price to be located in good locations. Purchaser will hold tickets till afternoon of show at which time Producer will release all tickets he does not plan to use.

    b) Purchaser shall be responsible to pay the Producer its percentage for every seat occupied within the place of performance.

    c) All percentage payments provided for hereunder shall be paid to the respective Producer or representative and shall be accompanied with a signed written statement from the Purchaser.

    d) All prices for tickets, the scaling of the house, and any and all discounting of tickets must be approved by the Producer. Such approval shall not be unreasonably withheld.

    e) Purchaser further agrees to have on hand at the place of engagement the night of the show, for counting and verification by a representative of Producer, all unsold tickets. Producer shall be compensated for the difference between the number of tickets manifested. If the Purchaser shall violate any of the proceeding provisions of the paragraph, it shall be deemed that Purchaser has sold a ticket for each seat in the house (and permitted standing room) at the highest ticket price for which the house is scaled.

f) Purchaser further agrees to give said representative the right to enter the box office at any time (during the performance and after the performance) and to examine and make extracts from the box office records of Purchaser relating to the gross receipts of this engagement. A written box office statement certified and signed by the Purchaser will be furnished.

g) Purchaser may not sell tickets to performance herein as part of a series of other concerts without prior written consent of Producer. All tickets printed under the manifest shall be of the one stub, one price variety. There shall be no multiple price tickets printed. Examples of tickets prohibited under this agreement are:
   (1) One price for students and different price for general admission on the same ticket, or;
   (2) One price for tickets bought in advance and a different price for tickets bought at the gate on the same ticket.

h) If the Purchaser violates the above agreement, he shall be liable for the total amount of tickets sold at the highest price printed on the tickets. All tickets shall be printed by a bonded ticket house (example: Globe Tickets, Arcus-Simples) or, if the performance is at a college or university, the official printing department of the university or college.

i) Purchaser agrees that if there is any discrepancy in the accounting for the show in tickets, monies, or related areas, the show will be called a sellout, and all monies will be paid accordingly, before the Producer performance. The Purchaser may redeem any monies due him only with an audit by a certified public accountant or the U.S. Internal Revenue Department.

j) Purchaser agrees not to discount tickets or to offer tickets as a premium without first obtaining permission in writing from Producer. If Producer does sell or distribute discount complimentary tickets without such prior approval or in excess of the number permitted, he shall be liable for the full ticket price of each such ticket sold or distributed.

F4. This agreement shall not be construed to create a joint venture or partnership between Purchaser and Producer and no business relationship other than that of Purchaser/Producer shall exist between the parties.

F5. Purchaser agrees that Producer may cancel the engagement hereunder by giving the Purchaser written notice thereof at least thirty (30) days prior to the commencement date of the engagement hereunder, if Producer shall be called upon to render services in connection with theatrical motion picture(s), television, or a legitimate stage play and if the engagement hereunder might conflict therewith.

F6. In the event of public calamity or riots, epidemic, fire, serious illness or injury, cancellation not under the control of Producer, or other act of God, no claim shall be made of Producer in respect of non-fulfillment of this Agreement with regard to the concert(s) so effected. In the event of serious illness or injury, a Doctor's certificate will be supplied by Producer.

F7. In the event Purchaser shall breach this agreement, Producer shall have the right without limiting any of its other remedies hereunder to refrain from rendering a performance or to stop rendering a performance if such breach occurs during the rendition of a performance. Notwithstanding the cessation of such performance, Purchaser shall be liable to Producer for all of the fees and compensation hereunder in the same manner though Producer had fully performed. A BREACH OF ANY CLAUSE CONTAINED IN THIS RIDER BY THE PURCHASER SHALL BE DEEMED A MATERIAL BREACH. If Producer elects to perform or continue to perform notwithstanding a breach of this agreement by Purchaser, the performance by Producer shall not constitute a waiver or any claim the Producer may have for damages or otherwise.

F8. This agreement may not be changed, modified, or altered except by an instrument in writing by the parties. This agreement shall be construed in accordance with the laws of the State of California. Any claim or dispute arising out of or relating to this agreement or the breach thereof shall be settled by arbitration in California.

F9. Any proposed additional terms and conditions which may be affixed to this contract by Purchaser does not become part of this contract until signed by Producer. By sole act of signing,

Purchaser readily accepts all provisions of Producer's contract, regardless of any additions or deletions he may try to make.

F10. Artists assume no personal liability for any act or omission of Producer, or employees of Producer.

F11. The above constitutes the sole, complete and binding agreement between the parties hereto.

ACCEPTED AND AGREED TO:

DATE _____ DATE _____

_____ _____
PURCHASER   PRODUCER

PROMOTER'S RIDER

RIDER AGREEMENT dated _____, between the Promoter, and _____, hereinafter called the Artist.

1. It is clearly understood and agreed that the foregoing agreement does not constitute an employer-employee relationship, that Artist is acting solely hereunder as an independent contractor and shall be solely responsible for all so-called "Employer Contributions" including without limitation unemployment, withholding and similar contributions or payroll charges. In the event that Artist's services are furnished by a corporation, said corporation warrants and represents that the Artist is covered by workmen's compensation insurance and disability benefits and that said corporation is solely responsible for all "Employer Contributions".

2. Artist is also responsible for all hotel and travel expenses of himself and his group, if any, unless specified on the face of contract.

3. Artist expressly assumes all risk inherent to the rendition of Artist's service hereunder, and releases the Promoter from all liability therefore including, without limitation, risk of injury to the Artist and his personal property while engaged in any activities pursuant to this contract, except such as may be due to negligence of the Promoter.

4. Artist understands that other artists may be included on the

program. Therefore, if Artist fails to appear or perform all or any of the performances scheduled hereunder, other than for illness or Act of God, Artist shall pay the Promoter his pro-rata share of all sums of money expended in connection with the advertising, promotion and payment of other acts for the date scheduled hereunder, taking into account the other artists scheduled to appear at the same performance.

5. It is further understood and agreed that upon cancellation by the Artist, the Artist shall not perform or appear within a sixty (60) mile radius of city of engagement until such date when the Artist shall perform for the Promoter at the same price and upon the same conditions as contained herein, at the option of the Promoter which option shall be exercised in writing within twenty (20) days after the first scheduled date.

6. In the event of riot, civil disorder, Acts of God, periods of national mourning, rebellions, bomb threats necessitating the cancellation of the concert, or floods, tornadoes, hurricanes, or any other natural disaster which causes the area in which the concert site is located to be declared a national disaster are eligible for federal aid, the Promoter shall have the authority to cancel this agreement without further obligation between the parties hereto, except that in the event of such cancellation, all deposits paid hereunder shall be immediately refunded to the Promoter.

7. Artist shall not appear within a sixty (60) mile radius of city of engagement sixty (60) days prior to and thirty (30) days after date of performance without written permission from the Promoter. Permission will not be unreasonably withheld. In the event that any third party advertises or acts in violation of this agreement, Artist agrees to join the Promoter as a party plaintiff to enjoin said acts.

8. Artist warrants that he will not conduct his performance in any area other than on the stage provided by the Promoter. Artist further warrants that he shall not deliberately encourage vocally or by hand or body movements members of the audience to leave their assigned seating areas. In the event Artist breaches any of the foregoing warranties, the Promoter shall be entitled to withhold, as liquidated damages, any additional sums to be paid to Artist for such engagement pursuant to this contract. The foregoing sentence shall not impair or otherwise

diminish the right of the Promoter to recover such larger damages as it shall suffer or prove or limit or restrict any other legal or equitable remedy available to it due to Artist's breach of the foregoing warranties. Artist will generally conduct himself in such a manner or rendition of his services hereunder and he does therefore indemnify the Promoter from and against all claims of third parties resulting from breach of warrant, including the reasonable costs of defending against such claims.

9. Artist agrees that starting time on the face of the contract is the time Artist and members of his group should be present at the site of engagement, unless otherwise notified by the Promoter. Artist will be notified of performance time within twenty one (21) days of engagement date.

10. Unless stipulated on the face of the contract, the Promoter will have the sole right to determine position of Artist on the show. Because there may be several artists appearing, no program or souvenir merchandise may be sold on behalf of the Artist without written consent of the Promoter.

11. Artist will be ready to appear as scheduled by the Promoter. Artists who appear late or who are otherwise not ready to appear at the time assigned may be reassigned to a different time in the program in the absolute discretion of the Promoter; such rescheduling shall not limit any of the Promoter's other rights or remedies in the event of Artist's breach of Artist's obligation to appear and be ready at the originally scheduled time.

12. Promoter shall be entitled to permit photo coverage and news film coverage of the event for general news purposes. Promoter will impose a two minute limitation upon such film footage as may be taken for such general news purposes. Artist also agrees to be available for TV, radio and newspaper interviews.

PROMOTER

_____

_____   _____
BY: ARTIST

APPENDIX E
CARNET INFORMATION

CARNETS MAY BE ISSUED FOR USE IN THE FOLLOWING COUNTRIES:

Australia	Hungary	Norway
Austria	Iceland	Poland
Belgium	Iran	Portugal
Bulgaria	Ireland	Rumania
Canada*	Israel	South Africa
Cyprus	Italy	Spain
Czechoslovakia	Ivory Coast	Sweden
Denmark	Japan	Switzerland
Finland	Korea, Republic of	Turkey
France	Luxembourg	United Kingdom
Germany	The Netherlands	United States
Greece	New Zealand	Yugoslavia
Hong Kong		

*Certain professional equipment not accepted.

CARNETS CAN BE OBTAINED FROM THE U.S. COUNCIL OF THE INTERNATIONAL CHAMBER OF COMMERCE AT THE FOLLOWING OFFICES:

U.S. Council of the
   International Chamber of Commerce Inc.
1212 Avenue of the Americas
New York, N.Y. 10036
(212) 354-4480

U.S. Council of the
   International Chamber of Commerce Inc.
3345 Wilshire Boulevard
Los Angeles, CA 90010
(213) 386-0767

U.S. Council of the
 International Chamber of Commerce Inc.
700 Nicholas Boulevard
Elk Grove Village, IL 60007
(312) 364-7838

U.S. Council of the
 International Chamber of Commerce Inc.
100 California Street
Suite 1100
San Francisco, CA 94111
(415) 956-3356

INDEX

Agents, 79, 82
Aircraft, comparison of, 35–36
Air freight
   packing equipment for, 55
   procedures, 56–57
   rates, 57
Airlines
   boarding procedures, 31–32
   "bumping," compensation for, 31
   cancellations and delays, 30–31
   checking in, 23–24
   commuter airlines, 35
   comparison of, 36–39
   complaints, 37
   discount fares, 17–19
   excess baggage charges, 24–27, 34
   flight insurance, 34–35, 102
   international, 37–39
   lost baggage, 28–30
   Official Airline Guide, 39–40
   refunds, 22–23
   reservations, 16–17, 32
   tickets, 20–23
Automobile Association of America, 52

Bus, charter, 43

Canada
   customs, 89–90
   manifest of all tour members, 90
   security deposit on equipment, 89–90
   withholding tax, 90–91
Cancelling a performance, 81, 82–83
Car insurance, 116–118
Car leasing, 50–51
Car loan, 116
Carnet, 59, 88, 107–109
Car rental
   credit card, 102–103
   discount, 52, 102–103
   firms, 43–45
   foreign, 49
   insurance, 48
   rates, 46
   repairs, 47
   reservations, 47–48

   through *Airlines Passengers Association*, 40
Car repair kit, 51
Cashier's check, 96, 98–99
Certified check, 96–97
Charter flights, 39
Concorde, 39
Contracts
   negotiation, 80–81
   riders, 81–82
   when to cancel, 81, 82–83
Credit cards, 100–104
Credit rating, establishing, 115
Credit unions, 115
Currency, changing, 75, 89, 97–98
Customs
   brokers, 60
   carnet, 108–109
   freight, 59
   office hours, 56

Equipment
   adapters, 86–87
   carnet, 107–108
   cases, 55
   hotel security, 67
   on tour, 84–85
   oversized, 27
   rental, 85
   repair, 85–86
   shipping, 55–60, 24–27
   transformers, 86–87
Eurail pass, 43
Europe
   maps and guides, 51–52
   trains, 42–43
   hotels, 73–75
Expense reports, 106–107

Foreign tours
   Canada, 89–91
   carnet, 88
   carrying cash, 98
   electrical problems, 86–87
   hotels, 73–75
   mail, 100
   passports, 87
   sending money home, 99
   visas, 87–88

work permits, 87–88
Freight forwarders, 59

Guidebooks, travel, 51–52
Guitar, as airline baggage, 26

Holiday Inns, 2
Hotels, see *Lodging*.

Instruments, as airline baggage, 26
Insurance
  baggage, 28–29
  car, 116–118
  car rental, 48
  flight insurance, 34–35, 102
  from AAA, 52
  health, 120
  property, 119–120
  travel, 119
International driver's license, 52

Limousine service, 50
Lodging
  airport hotels, 65
  checking in and out, 72, 73
  foreign, 73–75
  hotel/motel chains, 63–64
  hotel services, 73
  long term, 72
  rates, 68–70, 71–72
  reservations, 71
Luggage, 27–28

Mail service, 99–100
Managers, 79, 82
Maps, 51–52
Mexico, driving in, 47
Milan airport, 24
Money
  carrying cash across borders, 98–99
  changing currency, 75, 89
  hotel safe deposit boxes, 96
  payments, 80, 83–84
Money order, Western Union, 95
Musicians union, 110–11

Passports, 87
Promoters, 79–80, 82

Rent-a-Wreck, 45

Safe deposit boxes, 96
Skycap service, 25

Taxes, 106–107
Taxis, 50
Telegrams, 105–106
Telephone
  credit calls, 103
  Europe/transatlantic, 105
Telex, 106
Trains
  baggage, 41–42
  Europe, 42–43
  Japan, 42
  reservations, 41
  tickets, 42
Travel agents, 15–16, 64
Truck rental, 49–50
Traveler's checks, 97, 98–99

Van rental, 44
Visas, 87–88
VIP lounges, 34

Western Union money order, 95
Work permits
  Canada, 89
  Europe, Japan, 87–88